FIRST
FACTS
ABOUT
U.S.
HISTORY

Published by Blackbirch Press, Inc.
260 Amity Road
Woodbridge, CT 06525

© 1996 Blackbirch Press, Inc.
First Edition

Printed in China

10 9 8 7 6 5 4

Library of Congress Cataloging-in-Publication Data

King, David C.
    First facts about U.S. history / by David C. King
      p.   cm. — (First facts about ...)
    Includes bibliographical references and index.
    Summary: Introduces significant people and events in American history from colonial
times to the 1990s.
    ISBN 1-56711-168-8 (lib bdg. : alk. paper)
    1. United States—History—Juvenile literature. [1. United States—History.] I. Title.
II. Series: First facts about ...
(Woodbridge, Conn.)
E178.3.K5 1996
973—dc20   95-38259
                                                               CIP
                                                                AC

FIRST FACTS ABOUT

U.S. HISTORY

by

David C. King

BLACKBIRCH PRESS, INC.

WOODBRIDGE, CONNECTICUT

Contents

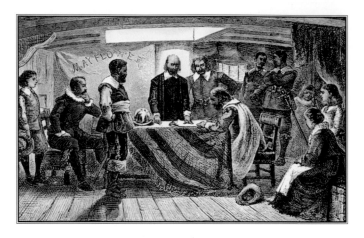

Colonial America

*T*he United States of America is a nation created by a great mixing of peoples, cultures, and ideas from different parts of the world. That mixing began about 500 years ago, when the countries of Europe started to finance expeditions to explore distant regions of the globe. Portugal, Spain, Great Britain, and other nations developed ships that could sail across the oceans. The Europeans learned about gunpowder from the Chinese and used it in guns and cannons.

Native Americans lived in North America long before Europeans arrived.

Their sturdy ships and their powerful weapons gave Europeans a big advantage over other peoples. From the 1400s to the 1800s, they gained control over much of the world.

In 1492, Christopher Columbus, an Italian who was sailing for the king and queen of Spain, accidentally reached what would become known as "the Americas." North America and South America were a "New World" to the Europeans, because they had not known that these two continents existed. But other people had been living on these lands for thousands of years. Columbus named them "Indians," believing that he had landed on a group of islands in Asia called the Indies. The Indians—or Native Americans—were really the first Americans.

Christopher Columbus was not the first European to have reached the Americas. In about 1000—five centuries before his 1492 voyage—a band of hardy seafarers landed on the northeast coast of present-day Canada. They were Vikings, or Norsemen, from the northern region of Europe that is now Norway and Sweden. They stayed for three years, calling the place Vinland because of its many grape vines. But they never knew that they had reached the edge of a vast continent.

Spain, however, built a huge empire in this New World. The empire, "New Spain," covered Mexico and much of present-day Central and South America, as well as islands in the Caribbean Sea. The Spanish also explored and claimed Florida and what is now the southwestern United States. Gold, silver, and other riches from the empire made Spain wealthy and powerful.

Rulers of other countries envied Spain. In the late 1500s, France, the Netherlands, and Great Britain started to settle colonies in the Americas. The newcomers were attracted to North America because Spain did not control very much of it. Much of the area that the British explored and settled would one day become the United States.

c. 1000 Vikings reach the northeast coast of present-day Canada

1492 Christopher Columbus arrives in the "New World"

1513 Juan Ponce de León searches for the fountain of youth on a peninsula that he names Florida

1519–1521 The Spanish, led by Hernando Cortés, conquer the Aztec Empire

1540–1542 Francisco Vásquez de Coronado explores what is now known as the American Southwest

1565 St. Augustine is established

1587 The colony of Roanoke is settled by the British

1607 Jamestown is settled

1619 The House of Burgesses is established

Africans are brought to Virginia to work as indentured servants

1620 The Pilgrims establish the Plymouth colony in present-day Massachusetts

1621 The first Thanksgiving is celebrated

1630 Massachusetts Bay Colony is founded by the Puritans

1664 The British take over the Dutch colony of New Netherland; it becomes the colonies of New York and New Jersey

1681 William Penn invites people of all religions to come live in the new colony of Pennsylvania

1732 Benjamin Franklin publishes the first edition of *Poor Richard's Almanac*

1755 The French and Indian War begins

1759 The British capture Quebec

1763 Ottawa chief Pontiac leads a rebellion against the British

The Treaty of Paris ends the French and Indian War

A "NEW WORLD"

THE FIRST EUROPEANS

In this painting, Christopher Columbus is shown landing in the "New World."

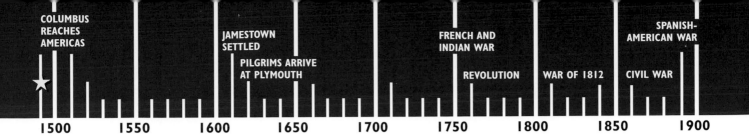

| COLUMBUS REACHES AMERICAS | JAMESTOWN SETTLED | | FRENCH AND INDIAN WAR | | | SPANISH-AMERICAN WAR |
| | PILGRIMS ARRIVE AT PLYMOUTH | | REVOLUTION | WAR OF 1812 | CIVIL WAR | |

1500   1550   1600   1650   1700   1750   1800   1850   1900

- 1492 Christopher Columbus reaches the Americas
- 1513 Juan Ponce de León explores Florida
- 1519-1521 Hernando Cortés seizes Aztec wealth for Spain
- 1540-1542 Francisco Vásquez de Coronado explores what is now the southwestern part of the United States
- 1565 St. Augustine is established

On October 12, 1492, a Spanish ship dropped anchor off a small island in the Caribbean Sea. Christopher Columbus, an Italian navigator sailing for the king and queen of Spain, had traveled west from Europe across the Atlantic Ocean and reached the Americas. Columbus, however, thought that he had reached the Indies, a group of islands in Asia. The goal of his voyage had been to find a western sea route to the Indies, China, and Japan, opening a rich trade in such things as silk, tea, spices, ivory, and jade.

Within a few years, other explorers found that Columbus had really stumbled upon two continents that had been unknown to Europeans. Asia was still half a world away. A mapmaker named this "New World" America, after one of the explorers—Amerigo (or Americus) Vespucci.

Europeans quickly realized that the continents of North and South America held great wealth. In 1519, in present-day Mexico, the Spanish, led by Hernando Cortés, began their conquest of the Aztec Empire, an ancient civilization. Later, another Spanish force conquered the Inca Empire, in South America. From these two conquests, ship after ship loaded with treasure made its way back to Spain. Two great Native-American civilizations had been overwhelmed by European power, setting a tragic pattern that would be repeated over and over again throughout the New World.

SPANISH FLORIDA

In 1513, a Spanish explorer named Juan Ponce de León heard that a "fountain of youth" existed. He set out to find it. Ponce de León explored a peninsula that he named Florida. In Spanish, *Florida* means "land of flowers." Ponce de León never found his fountain, but he did claim the area for Spain. In 1565, Spanish settlers went to Florida and established St. Augustine. Today, St. Augustine is the oldest city in the United States.

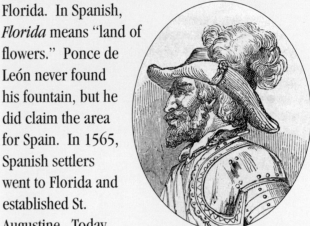

Juan Ponce de León explored Florida during his search for a fountain of youth.

HORSES ON THE GREAT PLAINS

Another Spanish explorer claimed what is now the American Southwest for Spain. From 1540 to 1542, Francisco Vásquez de Coronado and his men traveled as far north as present-day Kansas, searching for legendary "cities of gold," which turned out to be Native-American villages. On the journey, some of the Spaniards' horses ran away. The animals thrived on the lush grasses of the Great Plains and multiplied into large, wild herds. Over the next 200 years, some Native-American peoples developed great skill in training and riding the animals. By the time American pioneers reached the Great Plains in the 1800s, such tribes as the Sioux and Comanche depended on horses for warfare and for hunting.

9

SETTLING JAMESTOWN

THE FIRST PERMANENT BRITISH COLONY

Captain John Smith of the Jamestown Colony.

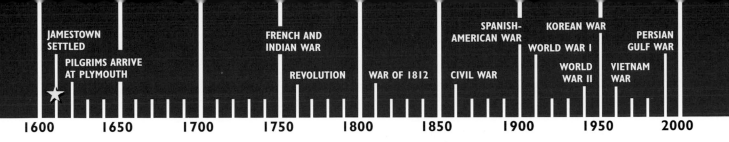

JAMESTOWN SETTLED

PILGRIMS ARRIVE AT PLYMOUTH

FRENCH AND INDIAN WAR

REVOLUTION

WAR OF 1812

CIVIL WAR

SPANISH-AMERICAN WAR

KOREAN WAR

WORLD WAR I

WORLD WAR II

VIETNAM WAR

PERSIAN GULF WAR

1600   1650   1700   1750   1800   1850   1900   1950   2000

- **1587-1590 The "Lost Colony" of Roanoke is settled—and vanishes**
- **1607 Jamestown is settled**
- **1619 The first legislature in British America is established**
  The first Africans are brought to British America

The settlers arrive at Jamestown.

In 1607, more than a century after New Spain was established, three British ships landed 104 men and boys on the banks of the James River, in present-day Virginia. They started a settlement that they named Jamestown, in honor of King James I of England.

The colonists had come hoping to find gold or some other source of quick wealth. Instead, they found themselves in a grim struggle for survival. Fifty of the settlers died from disease and starvation in their first five months there. Then a strong-willed man named Captain John Smith took charge. He forced the settlers to build huts and a fort, instead of hunting for gold. Native Americans showed the colonists how to plant corn and brought them wild turkey and deer. With this help, the settlement survived a "starving time."

The Jamestown settlers also learned of another Native-American crop—tobacco. This crop became an important source of income for the colonists. In 1619, the colony, by then named Virginia, established a lawmaking body, or legislature. Called the House of Burgesses, it marked the beginning of self-government in British America.

THE LOST COLONY

In 1587—20 years before Jamestown—117 British settlers had landed on Roanoke Island, off the coast of present-day North Carolina. The colony started well enough, and a child was even born—Virginia Dare, the first child to be born of European parents in British America. The colonists' ship went back to England for supplies. But when it returned in 1590, all the settlers had disappeared. Their belongings were in disarray, but no dead bodies or skeletons were found. The mystery of what happened to the people of the "Lost Colony" of Roanoke has never been solved.

THE BEGINNING OF SLAVERY

In 1619, a Dutch ship brought 20 Africans to Virginia. This marked the opening of a tragic chapter in American history. These Africans were indentured servants, who would be free after a period of time. But by the 1640s, Africans were being sold as slaves. Taken from their homeland and transported to America against their will, these immigrants were to play an important part in the story of the United States.

Landing Africans at Jamestown from a Dutch warship.

11

PILGRIMS AND PURITANS

SETTLERS IN NEW ENGLAND

The *Mayflower* carried the first European settlers to New England.

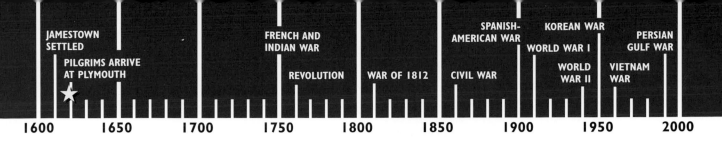

JAMESTOWN SETTLED		FRENCH AND INDIAN WAR		SPANISH-AMERICAN WAR	KOREAN WAR	PERSIAN GULF WAR
PILGRIMS ARRIVE AT PLYMOUTH				WORLD WAR I	
		REVOLUTION	WAR OF 1812	CIVIL WAR	WORLD WAR II	VIETNAM WAR

| 1600 | 1650 | 1700 | 1750 | 1800 | 1850 | 1900 | 1950 | 2000 |

- 1620 The Pilgrims establish Plymouth, the first New England colony
- 1621 The Pilgrims hold the first celebration of "thanksgiving"
- 1630 The Puritans start Massachusetts Bay Colony
- 1636-1638 Rhode Island and Connecticut Colonies are founded
- 1679 Settlers in New Hampshire form a separate colony

On November 11, 1620, after two months spent crossing the stormy Atlantic Ocean, a small English ship dropped anchor off the tip of Cape Cod in what is now known as the state of Massachusetts. Many of the *Mayflower*'s 102 passengers were colonists searching for a place to establish their own church—separate from the Church of England. They called themselves Pilgrims.

In December, the Pilgrims moved across Cape Cod Bay and established the settlement of Plymouth. Like the settlers at Jamestown, the Pilgrims faced a "starving time." Half of them died during that first hard winter. They were saved by a member of the Pawtucket tribe named Squanto. He showed the settlers how to fish and taught them how to grow Native-American foods—corn, squash, pumpkins, and beans. In November 1621, the Pilgrims celebrated their survival in the new land with a feast of "thanksgiving." That celebration became an annual tradition in the United States.

In 1630, a larger group of British settlers established the nearby colony of Massachusetts Bay. Called Puritans—because they wanted to "purify" the Church of England—they sought religious freedom. The first year was very difficult, but over the next ten years, more than 20,000 British settlers came to live in Massachusetts Bay. The colony thrived and later absorbed Plymouth.

The Mayflower Compact is signed.

THE MAYFLOWER COMPACT

The *Mayflower* was supposed to take the Pilgrims to Virginia Colony, but storms forced the ship to land far to the north. The Pilgrims realized that they were outside the region governed by British laws. Before going ashore, therefore, they drew up and signed an agreement that became known as the Mayflower Compact. In this compact, the colonists agreed to make their own laws and to obey those laws. The Mayflower Compact helped to establish the idea that people should have a voice in their government.

THE NEW ENGLAND COLONIES

The Puritans of Massachusetts Bay Colony did not welcome anyone whose religious beliefs were different from theirs. Two people who dared to express different views—Anne Hutchinson and Roger Williams—were banished from the colony. With their followers, they established new settlements, which became the colony of Rhode Island. Other colonists moved out of Massachusetts Bay in search of greater freedom and new land. This led to the founding of Connecticut, in 1636. In 1679, settlers who had moved north established the colony of New Hampshire.

13

THE THIRTEEN COLONIES

THE BEGINNINGS OF A NEW COUNTRY

Massachusetts Bay Colony.

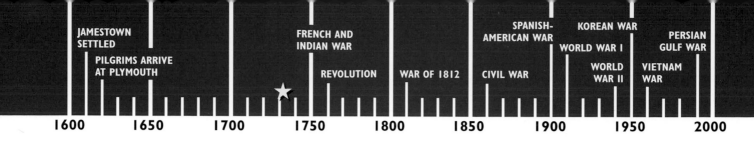

| JAMESTOWN SETTLED | | FRENCH AND INDIAN WAR | | | SPANISH-AMERICAN WAR | KOREAN WAR | PERSIAN GULF WAR |
| PILGRIMS ARRIVE AT PLYMOUTH | | REVOLUTION | WAR OF 1812 | CIVIL WAR | WORLD WAR I | WORLD WAR II | VIETNAM WAR |

| 1600 | 1650 | 1700 | 1750 | 1800 | 1850 | 1900 | 1950 | 2000 |

- **1634** Maryland is founded as a haven for Catholics
- **1664** New Netherland becomes New York and New Jersey
  The Carolinas are established
- **1681** William Penn founds Pennsylvania
- **1682** Delaware is founded
- **1732** Georgia is established as the 13th colony

Why would people in Great Britain and other parts of Europe risk a dangerous ocean crossing to settle in a land that was to them an untamed wilderness? For one thing, times were hard for people in Europe. Most could not buy land or find work. In addition, members of new religious groups were often jailed, or even executed, because their beliefs were unpopular. Imagine, then, what it would be like for these people to read a pamphlet written by William Penn in 1681 in which he promised that people of all religions would be welcome in his new colony of Pennsylvania. Each family would also receive some acres of land free and could buy more, he promised. To the thousands of immigrants who came to America each year, the colonies offered amazing freedoms and new opportunities.

By 1732, there were 13 British colonies. The New England Colonies—Massachusetts, Connecticut, Rhode Island, and New Hampshire—were made up of small farm villages and busy seaport towns such as Boston. In contrast, the Middle Colonies—New York, Pennsylvania, Delaware, and New Jersey—had larger farms that produced enough food to supply growing towns like Philadelphia and New York City. In the Southern Colonies—Maryland, Virginia, North and South Carolina, and Georgia—large plantations produced cash crops, such as tobacco and rice. As the plantations relied more on slave labor, the importing of slaves from Africa increased steadily.

The Dutch surrender New Amsterdam to the British.

NEW NETHERLAND

In the 1620s, the Dutch established the colony of New Netherland along the Hudson River. In 1664, four British warships sailed into the harbor of New Amsterdam (later named New York City) and demanded that the colony surrender. Dutch rule had been so unpopular that the Dutch settlers surrendered without a shot being fired. New Netherland became the colonies of New York and New Jersey, but the Dutch heritage would remain an important part of the American cultural mix.

THE FRENCH SETTLE IN NORTH AMERICA

At nearly the same time that Jamestown was established, French settlers started the fortress town of Quebec, in the land they called Canada. Later in the century, courageous French explorers traveled from the Great Lakes south to the mouth of the Mississippi River. They claimed this vast area for France and named it Louisiana, in honor of their king, Louis IV. Only a few thousand French settlers came to Canada (or "New France," as it was also known) or to Louisiana. By 1700, French rulers were satisfied that they had the English colonies hemmed in along the Atlantic coast.

THE GENIUS OF BEN FRANKLIN

The young colonial printer, Ben Franklin, in Philadelphia.

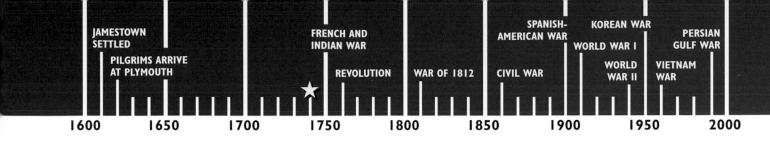

JAMESTOWN
SETTLED

PILGRIMS ARRIVE
AT PLYMOUTH

FRENCH AND
INDIAN WAR

REVOLUTION

WAR OF 1812

CIVIL WAR

SPANISH-
AMERICAN WAR

WORLD WAR I

KOREAN WAR

WORLD
WAR II

VIETNAM
WAR

PERSIAN
GULF WAR

1600   1650   1700   1750   1800   1850   1900   1950   2000

- **1706 Benjamin Franklin is born in
  Boston on January 17**
- **1732-1758 Franklin publishes *Poor
  Richard's Almanac***
- **1760-1790 Franklin is an important
  statesman in America and abroad**
- **1790 On April 17, at age 84, Franklin dies
  in Philadelphia**

When Benjamin Franklin arrived in Philadelphia, Pennsylvania, in 1723, he was 17 years old and almost penniless. He fell in love with the thriving city, with its bustling trade, its handsome brick buildings, and its people from many nations. Trained as a printer, Franklin soon had his own printing company and newspaper. He also wrote and published a best-selling almanac that he named *Poor Richard's Almanac*, which included his own wise and witty sayings. By his early 40s, Franklin was wealthy enough to retire from business and devote himself full-time to improving life in his city and colony.

Franklin applied his immense energy and talents to an amazing variety of tasks. He helped to give Philadelphia a public circulating library—the first of its kind in the world—and the first hospital in America. He organized a fire company and police force. Thanks to Franklin, the city was one of the first in the world to have paved streets and street lighting, using oil lamps that he had designed. He organized

The old library in Philadelphia.

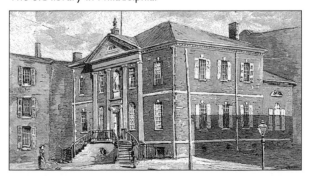

Pennsylvania's militia and started an academy that would become the University of Pennsylvania.

Franklin also gained worldwide fame as a scientist and inventor. His experiments laid the foundation for the modern science of electricity. His inventions included the Franklin stove, the lightning rod, and bifocal glasses. And during the last 30 years of his life, Franklin, as a respected scholar and statesman, played an important part in the American Revolution and the creation of the United States government.

THE POSTAL SYSTEM

In the early 1700s, mailing a letter was a risky business. Travel was slow—for example, it took a stagecoach six days to travel from Boston to New York. In addition, people paid cash for their mail when they received it, and dishonest post riders often overcharged them. And nosy neighbors thought nothing of opening and reading other people's mail. Benjamin Franklin served as postmaster of Philadelphia and was named the postmaster general by the Continental Congress. Under his guidance, mail delivery in America became much more efficient.

MEDICINE IN THE NEW WORLD

Until the mid-1800s, little was known about the causes and cures of disease. Epidemics of some diseases, such as smallpox and yellow fever, might take the lives of up to half the people in a stricken town. One of the most common treatments for any ailment was "bleeding"—drawing off the patient's blood to remove the "ill humors." But with the help of Native Americans, the colonists learned to use herbs and roots to make many useful medicines. Franklin's press printed many books describing how to make and use these remedies.

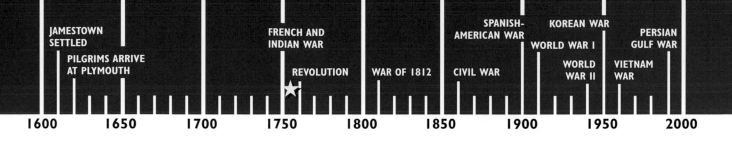

JAMESTOWN SETTLED

PILGRIMS ARRIVE AT PLYMOUTH

FRENCH AND INDIAN WAR

REVOLUTION

WAR OF 1812

CIVIL WAR

SPANISH-AMERICAN WAR

KOREAN WAR

WORLD WAR I

WORLD WAR II

PERSIAN GULF WAR

VIETNAM WAR

1600   1650   1700   1750   1800   1850   1900   1950   2000

- **1755–1763 The French and Indian War**
- **1759 The British capture Quebec, in French Canada**
- **1763 By the Treaty of Paris, France gives up nearly all its land in North America Pontiac's Rebellion is put down by British and colonial troops**

A battle on the Detroit River during the French and Indian War.

On July 9, 1755, a column of British troops and colonial militia marched into an ambush set by a combined force of Native-American warriors and French soldiers. Although the British and colonists were badly beaten that day, George Washington, a 23-year-old colonel in the Virginia militia, gained a reputation for bravery and leadership. Washington had two horses shot from under him, and four bullets ripped through his coat, but he coolly kept fighting and led his men to safety. This battle, fought on the western frontier of Pennsylvania, marked the beginning of the French and Indian War.

The war was part of a worldwide struggle for empire between France and Great Britain. In North America, the two nations clashed because both claimed the territory between the Appalachian Mountains and the Mississippi River. The French had managed to win the loyalty of many Native-American groups in the region by promising that they would not take over tribal lands.

Although they lost many battles in the early part of the war, the British and colonists managed to turn the tide. They forced the French to surrender. Later, in the Treaty of Paris of 1763, Canada became a British colony.

◄ George Washington and his men attack the French in the French and Indian War.

THE BATTLE OF QUEBEC

The decisive battle of the French and Indian War was the British capture of Quebec, in 1759. The major city of New France, Quebec was protected by a strong fort, which was located atop steep cliffs overlooking the St. Lawrence River. James Wolfe, a brilliant young British general, led a force up the face of the cliffs and overwhelmed the French defenders. Both Wolfe and the Marquis de Montcalm, the French commander, were killed in the battle.

PONTIAC'S REBELLION

When the French surrendered, Pontiac, a courageous chief of the Ottawa tribe, realized that the Native-American tribes would soon lose their lands to English colonists. He quickly forged an alliance of 18 tribes in the area south of the Great Lakes. For a few months in 1763, Pontiac's Rebellion blazed along the frontier. Pontiac's forces captured eight of the ten British forts and killed hundreds of settlers. The British and colonists finally managed to put down the uprising, but the rebellion showed that Native Americans would fight fiercely to hold onto their lands.

Pontiac, the great Ottawa leader.

The Road to Independence

With its victory over France in 1763, Great Britain became the world's most powerful country. Its navy ruled the oceans, and there were British colonies on every continent. But the war had been expensive, and the costs of maintaining this sprawling worldwide empire were enormous. The British Parliament and the king felt that it was only fair that the colonies pay their share of the expenses, so they placed new taxes on the colonists.

A meeting of American Patriots.

The colonists were furious. From the earliest days at Jamestown and Plymouth, they had become used to governing their own affairs. While each colony had a governor appointed by the king, it was the colonial assemblies, or legislatures, that passed laws and levied taxes. The colonists argued that, since they had no representatives in the Parliament, Britain had no right to tax them. "No taxation without representation" became the colonists' rallying cry.

The conflict over taxes became increasingly bitter. The colonists formed patriotic groups, such as the Sons of Liberty, and organized protests, such as boycotting, or refusing to buy, British goods. The British lifted some taxes, but they also imposed others. They stubbornly insisted on their right to control the American colonies.

In 1775, war erupted. One year later, the colonies declared their independence from Great Britain. How could the Thirteen Colonies hope to win against the mighty British Empire, with its powerful navy and large, professional army? One thing that weakened Britain was that many of its people did not want to fight against their fellow British subjects in the colonies. The American Patriots, on the other hand, were fighting for things they believed in—their homes and their basic rights.

The war lasted from 1775 to 1781. While the American forces were often defeated in battle, they had no intention of giving up. Finally, with help from France, Americans won their independence. The next task was to create a government that would unite the 13 independent "states"—as the colonies would be called—into a nation.

1763 King George III decrees that colonists cannot settle west of the
Appalachian Mountains

1770 Five colonists are killed by British redcoats

1773 Colonists dump British tea into the Boston Harbor in protest of the
British Tea Act

1774 Representatives from the colonies meet in Philadelphia for the
First Continental Congress

1775 The Battles of Lexington and Concord begin the American Revolution

The Second Continental Congress meets and forms the Continental
Army—George Washington is placed in command

The Battle of Bunker Hill takes place

1776 Thomas Paine publishes *Common Sense*

Thomas Jefferson writes most of the Declaration of Independence

The Second Continental Congress approves Jefferson's work on July 4

The British occupy New York City and Philadelphia

1777 The Patriots defeat the British in the Battle of Saratoga

George Washington's troops winter at Valley Forge

1781 Washington traps Cornwallis's troops at Yorktown, forcing the British
surrender, and puts an end to the Revolution

1783 The British sign the Treaty of Paris, recognizing American independence

1787 Delegates to the Constitutional Convention create the U.S. Constitution

1789 George Washington is elected president

1791 The Bill of Rights is ratified

THE BOSTON TEA PARTY

THE COLONISTS REBEL

The Boston Tea Party.

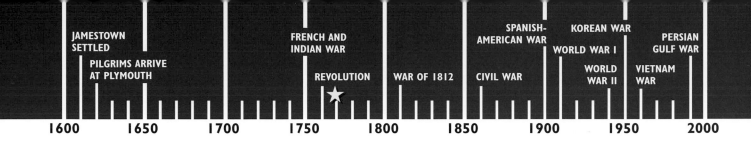

JAMESTOWN SETTLED
PILGRIMS ARRIVE AT PLYMOUTH
FRENCH AND INDIAN WAR
REVOLUTION
WAR OF 1812
CIVIL WAR
SPANISH-AMERICAN WAR
KOREAN WAR
WORLD WAR I
WORLD WAR II
PERSIAN GULF WAR
VIETNAM WAR

1600 1650 1700 1750 1800 1850 1900 1950 2000

- 1763 A royal proclamation closes the western lands
- 1764-1765 New British taxes anger the colonists
- 1770 The Boston Massacre takes place
- 1773 The British Tea Act leads to the Boston Tea Party
- 1774 Parliament passes the Intolerable Acts The First Continental Congress meets

In 1773, a dispute over tea set off a chain of events that was to lead to the American Revolution. To show that they had the power to control the American colonies, the British passed the Tea Act. This law meant that instead of buying untaxed tea, which was often smuggled in from other countries, the colonists would now have to buy their tea only from the British.

The colonists' answer to the Tea Act was the Boston Tea Party: On the night of December 16, 1773, a small group of Patriots, disguised as Native Americans, boarded three British ships and dumped 342 chests of British tea into the harbor at Boston, Massachusetts.

The British responded with a series of acts, or laws, designed to punish Massachusetts and warn the other colonies. These acts closed the port of Boston until the tea was paid for, took away much of the colony's self-government, and required the people of Massachusetts to house and feed British soldiers. But instead of frightening the colonists, these "Intolerable Acts," as the colonists called the laws, convinced them that united action was necessary. In September 1774, official delegates from 12 colonies met in Philadelphia, Pennsylvania, for the First Continental Congress. They called for a boycott of all British goods and for the militia of every colony to prepare for war. A furious King George III declared that Massachusetts was in a state of rebellion. The conflict had now reached the boiling point.

CLOSING THE WESTERN LANDS

The British government had been alarmed by the fury of Pontiac's Rebellion in 1763. King George III decided that the best way to avoid future trouble on the western frontier was to keep the colonists out. In the Proclamation of 1763, he announced that no settlers would be allowed west of the Appalachian Mountains. But many colonists felt that they had a right to move west. Frontiersman Daniel Boone even defied the king's order— he blazed the Wilderness Trail into the land called Kentucky.

THE BOSTON MASSACRE

One of the events that triggered bitter feelings against the British was an incident that became known as the Boston Massacre. The British had decided to station two regiments of redcoats—as British soldiers were called, because of their bright uniforms—in Boston. On March 5, 1770, a crowd of men and boys began taunting British guards. Tempers flared and shots were fired. Five of the colonists were killed, including a former slave named Crispus Attucks. The incident sent shock waves throughout the colonies. In pamphlets and speeches, Patriot leaders began using the Boston Massacre as a symbol of British tyranny.

The Boston Massacre.

LEXINGTON AND CONCORD

FIRST BATTLES OF THE REVOLUTION

The Battle of Lexington.

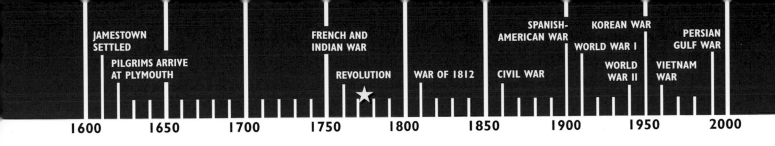

| JAMESTOWN SETTLED | | FRENCH AND INDIAN WAR | | | SPANISH-AMERICAN WAR | KOREAN WAR | | PERSIAN GULF WAR |
| PILGRIMS ARRIVE AT PLYMOUTH | | REVOLUTION | WAR OF 1812 | CIVIL WAR | | WORLD WAR I | WORLD WAR II | VIETNAM WAR |

1600   1650   1700   1750   1800   1850   1900   1950   2000

- 1775 **The American Revolution begins with the Battles of Lexington and Concord**
  The Second Continental Congress prepares for war
  George Washington is named commander-in-chief
  The Battle of Bunker Hill is fought

On the night of April 18-19, 1775, a regiment of British troops left Boston, Massachusetts, and marched inland. Their plan was to surprise the Patriots at Lexington and Concord, seize their supply of weapons, and capture two Patriot leaders. But the surprise failed, because Paul Revere and Billy Dawes rode through the night to warn the Patriots.

When the British redcoats reached Lexington, they were met by 70 "minutemen"—militia prepared to fight "at a moment's notice." Shots were fired, and eight colonists were killed and eight wounded. The British marched on to Concord, where they destroyed ammunition stores and skirmished with a larger Patriot force. When the redcoats started to return to Boston, they were caught in a deadly crossfire from minutemen hidden behind trees and stone walls along the line of march. Nearly 300 British soldiers were killed or wounded, compared to fewer than 100 colonists. These two battles marked the beginning of the American Revolution.

Militia units began swarming into the towns around British-controlled Boston. The Second Continental Congress met and formed the Continental Army, with George Washington as commander-in-chief. Members of the Congress were not yet ready to declare independence, but they were determined that the colonies would now fight for their rights.

THE BATTLE OF BUNKER HILL

The Battle of Bunker Hill.

Before Washington could reach Boston to take command, the Patriots fought their first full-scale battle against the British. On June 17, 1775, a force of 2,400 redcoats marched up Breed's Hill, overlooking Boston. They were met by a "sheet of fire" from 1,600 Patriots who had dug in the night before. After hours of bitter fighting, the British took the hill when the Patriots ran out of ammunition. They took Bunker Hill as well—the hill for which the battle was named. The Patriots lost a quarter of their troops, while the redcoats lost nearly half their attacking force. The colonial militia proved that day that it could hold its own against Britain's professional troops.

PATRIOTS AND LOYALISTS

There were 2.5 million people living in the Thirteen Colonies when the American Revolution began. Of this number, about 1 million were Patriots, who believed that they must fight the British for their rights. Another 1 million refused to take sides. And about 500,000 people remained loyal to Great Britain and the king. Tens of thousands of these Loyalists fought on the British side; many more fled to Canada or England.

THE DECLARATION OF INDEPENDENCE

FROM COLONIES TO STATES

A reproduction of the document that established the United States of America.

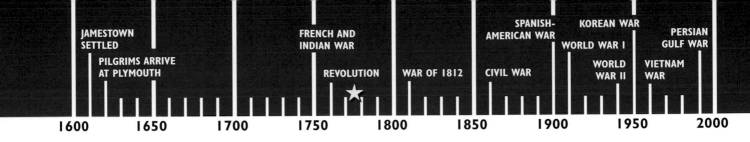

| JAMESTOWN SETTLED | | FRENCH AND INDIAN WAR | | | SPANISH-AMERICAN WAR | KOREAN WAR | | PERSIAN GULF WAR |
| PILGRIMS ARRIVE AT PLYMOUTH | | | REVOLUTION | WAR OF 1812 | CIVIL WAR | WORLD WAR I | WORLD WAR II | VIETNAM WAR |

1600   1650   1700   1750   1800   1850   1900   1950   2000

- **1776 Thomas Paine publishes his famous essay, *Common Sense***
  The British leave Boston on March 17
  The Second Continental Congress appoints a committee to draft a declaration of independence
  Congress approves the Declaration of Independence on July 4

The Second Continental Congress.

As George Washington organized the Continental Army outside Boston, he still proposed a toast each day to King George III. Most colonists shared Washington's feelings—although they were now at war, they still thought of themselves as British subjects.

Those feelings changed during the year following the Battles of Lexington, Concord, and Bunker Hill. By June 1776, the Second Continental Congress decided that only a complete break with Great Britain would protect Americans' rights. A committee was appointed to draft a declaration of independence. Thomas Jefferson of Virginia did most of the writing, using ideas from John Adams of Massachusetts and Benjamin Franklin of Pennsylvania.

In the document, Jefferson explained the reasons for declaring independence. All people, he wrote, have the right to "life, liberty, and the pursuit of happiness." If a government violates those rights, the people are justified in changing the government. Jefferson then listed all the grievances against the king, and concluded by declaring that "these United Colonies are, and of right ought to be, free and independent states."

On the evening of July 4, 1776, Congress approved the Declaration of Independence. The Thirteen Colonies had now become the 13 American states. The Declaration has ever since been a model to the world of a fundamental idea: that the government's power depends on the will of the people.

COMMON SENSE

In the early months of 1776, thousands of Patriots were reading a pamphlet called *Common Sense*, written by Thomas Paine. "In the following pages," Paine wrote, "I offer nothing more than simple facts, plain arguments, and common sense." Paine's pamphlet was a brilliant statement of why the struggling colonies should declare their independence from Britain. Within three months, 120,000 copies had been sold. Paine's powerful words had a strong influence on the decision to write the Declaration of Independence.

"ALL MEN ARE CREATED EQUAL...."

When Thomas Jefferson penned the words "All men are created equal" in the Declaration of Independence, he was well aware that the existence of slavery meant that all were not equal. Jefferson, however, believed in those words as an ideal, a goal toward which the nation should strive. In the years since 1776, "all men" has gradually come to include African Americans, Native Americans, women, and others who were once left out of the democratic system.

Thomas Jefferson

WINTER AT VALLEY FORGE

THE GENIUS OF WASHINGTON'S COMMAND

The brutal winter of 1777-1778 in Valley Forge.

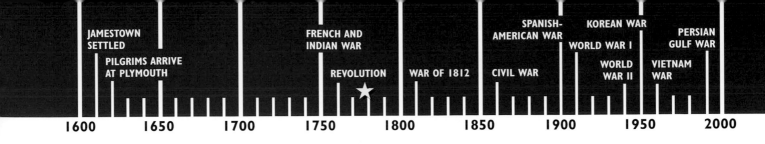

JAMESTOWN SETTLED

PILGRIMS ARRIVE AT PLYMOUTH

FRENCH AND INDIAN WAR

REVOLUTION

WAR OF 1812

CIVIL WAR

SPANISH-AMERICAN WAR

KOREAN WAR

WORLD WAR I

WORLD WAR II

VIETNAM WAR

PERSIAN GULF WAR

1600   1650   1700   1750   1800   1850   1900   1950   2000

- 1776 The British occupy New York City in September
  American victories at Trenton and Princeton
- 1777 The British occupy Philadelphia in September
  An American victory at Saratoga
- 1777-1778 Winter camp at Valley Forge, from December to June
- 1778 France forms an alliance with America

The American victory at the Battle of Princeton.

During the winter of 1777-1778, many people on both sides of the independence issue thought that the American cause was doomed to failure. The British had taken both New York City and Philadelphia, and George Washington's battered Continental Army endured a miserable winter at Valley Forge in Pennsylvania, not far from Philadelphia. While the British enjoyed the comforts of the two largest American cities, Washington's 11,000 men were often close to starvation. "They had neither coats, hats, shirts, or shoes," a French volunteer wrote. "Their feet and legs froze until they became black...." Perhaps as many as 3,000 Patriots died during that harsh winter.

In spite of the hardships, Washington's troops were actually gaining strength and confidence. They had great faith in their general. They had won battles at Trenton and Princeton in New Jersey, which convinced them that the enemy could be beaten. And, in October 1777, another Patriot army had soundly beaten the British in the Battle of Saratoga in New York.

At Valley Forge, Washington turned his men over to a German volunteer, Baron Friedrich von Steuben, for training. Von Steuben, a former officer in the Prussian Army, drilled the men hour after hour, day after day. By spring, the once-ragged Continental troops had become a proud, disciplined fighting force. When the British decided to leave Philadelphia in the spring of 1778, Washington's troops were ready to attack.

SARATOGA: THE TURNING POINT

The turning point in the Revolutionary War was the Battle of Saratoga, which lasted from September 19 to October 17, 1777. The British had tried a three-pronged attack to seize the Hudson River area, which would isolate New England from the other states. But bungling by the British and brilliant tactics by the Americans led to a stunning victory for the Americans. The battle convinced the French that the Americans could win, and they now entered the war against Britain. Benjamin Franklin, who went to France to represent America, helped to achieve this alliance. French troops, supplies, and warships played a vital role in the success of the American Revolution.

THE MARQUIS DE LAFAYETTE

Even before the alliance with France, a young French nobleman came to America and volunteered to serve in the Continental Army without pay. The Marquis de Lafayette, a former musketeer, was barely 20 years old, but Congress commissioned him as a major-general. Lafayette became close friends with George Washington, shared the suffering of Valley Forge, and served heroically in battle after battle.

VICTORY AT YORKTOWN

THE TREATY OF PARIS RECOGNIZES INDEPENDENCE

George Washington leads the Patriots against the British at Yorktown.

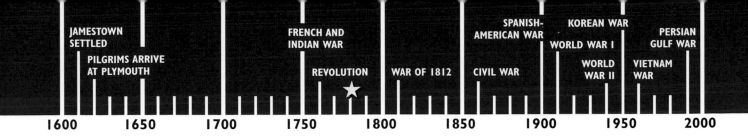

1600	1650	1700	1750	1800	1850	1900	1950	2000

JAMESTOWN SETTLED

PILGRIMS ARRIVE AT PLYMOUTH

FRENCH AND INDIAN WAR

REVOLUTION

WAR OF 1812

CIVIL WAR

SPANISH-AMERICAN WAR

KOREAN WAR

WORLD WAR I

WORLD WAR II

VIETNAM WAR

PERSIAN GULF WAR

- 1780 The British capture Savannah and Charleston
  The Americans are victorious at Kings Mountain
- 1781 An American victory at Cowpens
  In October, General Charles Cornwallis surrenders at Yorktown
- 1783 A peace treaty recognizes American independence

In the fall of 1781, every Continental soldier felt a keen sense of excitement as George Washington led them on a speedy and daring march south from New York. The men knew that a large British army under General Charles Cornwallis was trapped at Yorktown, Virginia, hemmed in by Patriot troops. After six years of warfare, this was their chance to clinch the final victory.

Since late in 1778, most of the fighting had shifted to the South. While Washington kept part of the British Army trapped in New York City, other British forces captured Savannah, Georgia, and then Charleston, South Carolina, where the Americans suffered their worst defeat of the war. But the Patriots fought back hard, using hit-and-run tactics, and Washington sent part of the Continental Army to help. After the Patriots had won pitched battles at Kings Mountain and Cowpens in North Carolina, Cornwallis moved his troops to Yorktown, on a peninsula in Chesapeake Bay. He expected reinforcements and help from the British Navy.

But Washington moved first. Patriot troops quickly blocked the neck of the peninsula. When a French fleet sailed into Chesapeake Bay, Cornwallis was trapped. In September 1781, Washington led a combined American and French force against Yorktown. After three weeks of steady bombardment, Cornwallis was forced to surrender, bringing the war to an end. In 1783, the British signed the Treaty of Paris, recognizing American independence.

Deborah Sampson   Molly Pitcher

WOMEN IN THE AMERICAN REVOLUTION

Women made many important contributions to the Patriot cause. For example, when a British force marched into Connecticut, 16-year-old Sybil Ludington made a daring 40-mile nighttime ride to summon troops. Sally St. Clair and Deborah Sampson dressed as men and marched into battle. Margaret Corbin and Molly Pitcher took over for their fallen husbands at their artillery posts. And many women, including Martha Washington, helped out in the army camps. Still others helped the Patriot cause by keeping family farms and businesses running throughout the war.

THE WAR AT SEA

Since the Continental Navy had only 13 ships, American warships never tried to attack the British fleets. But individual ships engaged in several heroic battles, marking the beginning of the American Navy's proud tradition. The most famous Patriot sea captain, John Paul Jones, even raided seacoast towns in Great Britain to give the British people a taste of the war. In addition, American privateers—armed merchant ships licensed to attack the enemy—captured more than 600 British cargo ships.

THE CONSTITUTION

CORNERSTONE OF FREEDOM

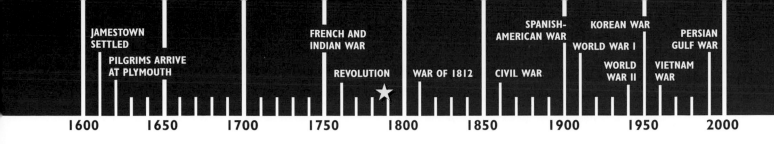

JAMESTOWN SETTLED

PILGRIMS ARRIVE AT PLYMOUTH

FRENCH AND INDIAN WAR

REVOLUTION

WAR OF 1812

CIVIL WAR

SPANISH-AMERICAN WAR

WORLD WAR I

KOREAN WAR

WORLD WAR II

PERSIAN GULF WAR

VIETNAM WAR

1600   1650   1700   1750   1800   1850   1900   1950   2000

- **1787 The Constitutional Convention draws up the Constitution**
- **1788 The Constitution is officially adopted**
- **1789 George Washington is elected the first president**
- **1791 The Bill of Rights is ratified**

During the summer of 1787, the windows of Philadelphia's Independence Hall were nailed shut. Inside, the 55 delegates to the Constitutional Convention put up with the ovenlike heat so that their deliberations could be secret.

Many outstanding leaders participated in the Convention, including George Washington and Benjamin Franklin. They were deeply divided over many issues, but after ten grueling weeks, they had produced the Constitution that continues to guide the nation to this day.

The Constitution created a federal system, made up of the individual states. The national (or federal) government was given certain powers, such as issuing money and dealing with other nations. Other powers were granted to the states.

After the Convention, the Constitution went to each state for ratification, or approval. The debate was fierce because many people feared that the strong national government would destroy individual rights. When supporters agreed to add a "bill of rights," the Constitution was ratified. The Bill of Rights, added in 1791 as the first Ten Amendments to the Constitution, guarantees such individual rights as freedom of speech, freedom of the press, and freedom of religion.

◄ The signing of the Constitution.

AMERICA'S FIRST WRITTEN CONSTITUTIONS

The long, bitter conflict with Great Britain had made the American people suspicious of government power. When independence was declared in 1776, the states quickly wrote state constitutions, spelling out exactly what their governments could and could not do. Most of these constitutions also included a bill of rights. In 1777, the Congress approved the Articles of Confederation, which provided a weak frame of government. The Articles gave the national government so little power that the 13 states could not really function as a nation. The need for a stronger government led to the Constitutional Convention of 1787.

THE NATION'S CAPITAL

When George Washington was inaugurated as the first president of the United States, on April 30, 1789, New York City was the nation's capital. Then, by an agreement between northern and southern members of Congress, work was begun on a new "federal city." Philadelphia served as the capital from 1790 to 1800, when the government moved to the new capital— Washington, D.C.

We the People

The Constitution.

33

Years of Growth and Change

*I*magine if George Washington could have come back to visit the United States in the year 1850—half a century after he had finished serving as the first president. He would have been astonished at how much the country had grown and changed. Instead of a nation of 4 million people living in 13 states along the Atlantic Coast, he now would have found 23 million people in 31 states stretching westward across the continent to the Pacific Ocean.

Members of the Lewis and Clark expedition meet Native Americans during their travels.

Washington also would have been amazed at how ways of living had changed. Inventors in Great Britain and the United States had learned to harness the power of rushing water and of steam. The result was a revolution in how things were made and how people traveled. Steamboats were plying the nation's rivers and, by the 1840s, steam railroads were speeding over the land.

In 1790, Samuel Slater, an immigrant from England, built a mill, or factory, at Pawtucket, Rhode Island. One of Slater's machines, powered by a water wheel, could spin 72 threads at a time. This was the start of the revolution in

how goods were made. By 1850, there were nearly 50,000 factories in the United States, mostly in the North. They churned out great quantities of fabrics, clocks, chairs, and dozens of other items.

For millions, this was a period of progress, abundance, and many new opportunities. But others found that the nation was falling far short of the Revolution's ideal of equality. Women in 1850 still could not vote or even own property. Native Americans were paying a heavy price for the nation's expansion; most of the eastern tribes had been forced to move west of the Mississippi River. And slavery, although now limited to the states of the South, had become more deeply entrenched than ever.

Eli Whitney's invention of the cotton gin had made cotton much more profitable to grow. In just a few years, it had become the nation's most important cash crop. The expansion of the South's "Cotton Kingdom" led to a renewed demand for slaves to work the fields. By 1850, more than 3 million African Americans lived in the bondage of slavery.

CHRONOLOGY

1793 Eli Whitney invents the cotton gin

1803 The United States buys the Louisiana Territory from France

Thomas Jefferson sends ships to challenge the Barbary pirates in Tripoli

1804 Meriwether Lewis and William Clark begin to explore western North America

1807 Robert Fulton's *Cleremont* travels up the Hudson River

1812 America goes to war against Britain

1814 British troops set fire to government buildings in Washington, D. C.

Francis Scott Key writes the "Star-Spangled Banner" after witnessing the bombardment of Fort McHenry

1815 General Andrew Jackson leads troops to victory at the Battle of New Orleans

1817 Construction begins on the Erie Canal

1821 Mexico wins independence from Spain

1836 Texans declare their independence from Mexico and declare the Republic of Texas

Davy Crockett and Jim Bowie fight General Antonio López de Santa Anna at the Alamo

1841 The first wagon train heads west to Oregon and California

1846 The United States declares war on Mexico

1848 Gold is discovered at Sutter's Mill in California

1850 California becomes a state

THE LOUISIANA PURCHASE

AMERICA DOUBLES ITS SIZE

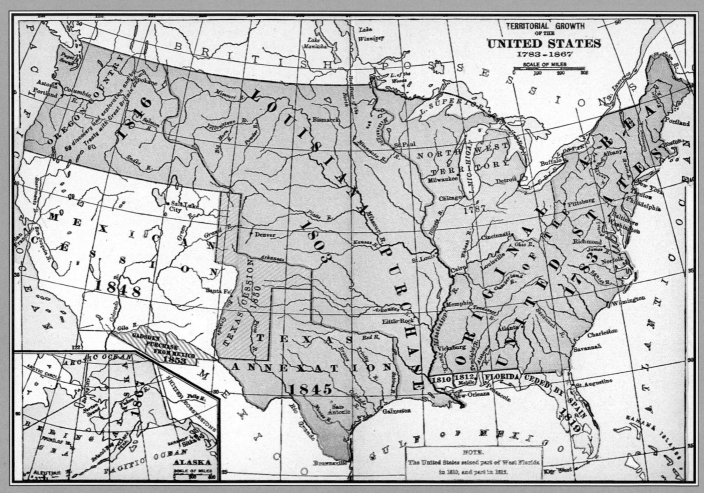

A map shows U.S. territorial growth during the 1800s.

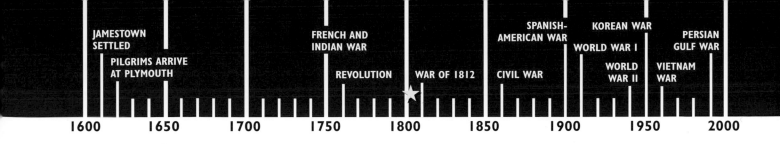

					SPANISH- AMERICAN WAR	KOREAN WAR	
JAMESTOWN SETTLED			FRENCH AND INDIAN WAR			WORLD WAR I	PERSIAN GULF WAR
PILGRIMS ARRIVE AT PLYMOUTH						WORLD WAR II	VIETNAM WAR
			REVOLUTION	WAR OF 1812	CIVIL WAR		

| 1600 | 1650 | 1700 | 1750 | 1800 | 1850 | 1900 | 1950 | 2000 |

- **1803 The United States buys the Louisiana Territory from France**
- **1804-1806 The Lewis and Clark expedition explores western North America**

In the country's early days, United States territory ended at the Mississippi River. The land to the west of the river was claimed by France. New Orleans, the port that controlled the mouth of the Mississippi, also belonged to France.

As Americans began to move west, however, they realized that the Mississippi was the key to the continent. Whoever controlled the river would also control access to the heartland of North America.

Thus, in 1803, President Thomas Jefferson sent representatives to France with an offer to buy New Orleans. The answer surprised him. Napoleon Bonaparte, the French ruler, offered to sell not just New Orleans but the entire Louisiana Territory—a vast wedge that covered well over 800,000 square miles—for $15 million.

Jefferson was not sure that the Constitution gave him the power to make such a purchase. But he and Congress agreed that the chance was too wonderful to miss. The Louisiana Purchase doubled the size of the United States. The price amounted to less than four cents an acre, making this one of the greatest real estate bargains of all time.

A portrait of Meriwether Lewis.

THE LEWIS AND CLARK EXPEDITION

Thomas Jefferson had long been fascinated by the unknown lands to the west of the United States. Even before the Louisiana Purchase was complete, he decided to send an expedition to explore the continent from the Mississippi

Meriwether Lewis's handwritten notes include a sketch of a trout.

River to the Pacific Ocean. He appointed two army officers—Captain Meriwether Lewis and Lieutenant William Clark—to lead it. They set out in May 1804. Guided by Sacajawea, a young Shoshone woman, they made their way across the Great Plains and through the Rocky Mountains. After 20 months of dangerous travel, Clark wrote in his journal, "Great joy! We are in view of the . . . great Pacific Ocean." The expedition then headed east again, arriving in St. Louis, Missouri, in September 1806.

THE BARBARY PIRATES

While Americans were beginning the westward push, the United States faced a challenge in the Mediterranean Sea. Pirates from four Barbary kingdoms in North Africa terrorized shipping routes, capturing ships and holding their crews for ransom. In 1803, President Jefferson sent warships to put an end to the piracy. After a brilliant raid led by Lieutenant Stephen Decatur, the pirates of Tripoli were defeated and agreed to peace. The other three Barbary states continued their piracy until Decatur was sent again in 1816.

THE WAR OF 1812

MORE CONFLICT WITH GREAT BRITAIN

The Battle of Lake Erie.

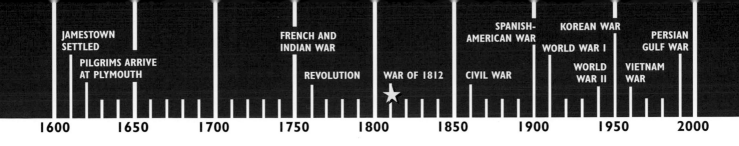

| JAMESTOWN SETTLED | | FRENCH AND INDIAN WAR | | | SPANISH-AMERICAN WAR | KOREAN WAR | | |
| PILGRIMS ARRIVE AT PLYMOUTH | | REVOLUTION | WAR OF 1812 | CIVIL WAR | WORLD WAR I | WORLD WAR II | VIETNAM WAR | PERSIAN GULF WAR |

| 1600 | 1650 | 1700 | 1750 | 1800 | 1850 | 1900 | 1950 | 2000 |

- 1812 The War of 1812 begins
- 1813 The American fleet wins the Battle of Lake Erie
- 1814 The British burn Washington, D.C.
        Americans win the Battle of Lake Champlain
        The Treaty of Ghent, declaring peace, is signed in December
- 1815 Americans win the Battle of New Orleans

In June 1812, less than 30 years after winning independence, Americans once again found themselves at war with Great Britain. The United States declared war mainly because of British interference with American ships. Americans were most outraged by the practice of impressment—taking sailors off American ships and forcing them to serve on British warships. Settlers on the western frontier also complained that the British, from their colony of Canada, were encouraging Native-American raids on outlying settlements.

The United States was unprepared for war, and three attempts to invade Canada were driven back. In 1814, British troops landed on the Atlantic Coast, marched into Washington, D.C., and set fire to most of the government buildings. American forces, however, managed to hold their own in other areas. They won important battles on Lake Erie and Lake Champlain. After 30 months of warfare, agents for the two sides signed a peace treaty in Ghent, Belgium. Before news of the peace arrived, American forces under General Andrew Jackson won the Battle of New Orleans, the greatest American victory of the war.

Although the war did not settle anything, it gave Americans a stronger sense of national pride and unity. And, from this time on, Great Britain treated the young nation with greater respect.

TECUMSEH: DEFENDER OF NATIVE-AMERICAN LANDS

"The once powerful tribes of our people," Tecumseh declared, were vanishing "as snow before a summer sun." To prevent the loss of more tribal lands to American settlers, Tecumseh, as Shawnee leader, called for a united force of all tribes. Although he hated war, he came to feel that his people must fight. But his supporters, led by his brother Tenskwatawa, known as the Prophet, were defeated in just one battle: the battle of Tippecanoe in Indiana, on November 7, 1811. Tecumseh then joined forces with the British in the War of 1812. He was killed in the Battle of the Thames in Upper Canada in 1813, ending the dream of Native-American unity.

THE STAR-SPANGLED BANNER

After the British burned Washington, D.C., they sailed toward Baltimore, Maryland. On September 13, 1814, they began a bombardment of Fort McHenry, which guarded the city. Francis Scott Key, a lawyer, watched the battle from a British warship, where he was trying to arrange an exchange of prisoners. At dawn, Key was thrilled to see a tattered American flat still flying above the fort. Inspired, he scribbled the lines of a poem, the "Star-Spangled Banner." Key's poem was printed in newspapers throughout the country and then set to music. Congress made it the official national anthem in 1931.

Francis Scott Key

THE ERIE CANAL

A NEW AGE FOR TRAVEL AND SHIPPING

Celebrators at the opening of the Erie Canal.

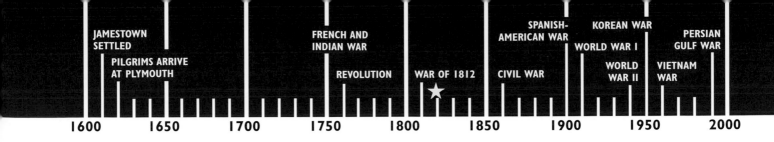

JAMESTOWN SETTLED

PILGRIMS ARRIVE AT PLYMOUTH

FRENCH AND INDIAN WAR

REVOLUTION

WAR OF 1812

CIVIL WAR

SPANISH-AMERICAN WAR

WORLD WAR I

KOREAN WAR

WORLD WAR II

VIETNAM WAR

PERSIAN GULF WAR

1600   1650   1700   1750   1800   1850   1900   1950   2000

- **1817 Construction begins on the Erie Canal**
- **1825 The entire canal is completed**
- **1830s-1850s The canal is periodically enlarged to handle the volume of traffic**

Governor DeWitt Clinton.

When, in 1817, New York governor DeWitt Clinton suggested building a canal connecting Lake Erie and the Hudson River, Thomas Jefferson called the idea "little short of madness." Many people agreed—the proposed 363-mile canal was soon nicknamed "Clinton's Big Ditch."

Clinton ignored the doubters and went ahead with construction. In 1825, he rode the first canal boat from Buffalo to Albany, then down the Hudson to New York City, where he dumped a keg of Lake Erie water into the Atlantic Ocean. The canal made travel so much easier that the price of shipping freight dropped. What had once cost $100 a ton to ship cost less than $10 in the 1850s. Settlers heading west could ride in comfort on barges pulled by horses or mules, passing through locks that raised or lowered the boats to different levels. Farmers in the Midwest could ship their products east for less and also pay less for eastern-manufactured goods.

The success of the Erie Canal touched off a canal-building craze. By 1840, more than 3,000 miles of canals connected major rivers and lakes. People could now travel from New York to the Gulf of Mexico on inland waterways.

ROADS AND TURNPIKES

In 1817, the year when the Erie Canal construction began, Congressman John C. Calhoun urged the nation to "bind the Republic together with a perfect system of roads and canals. Let us conquer space." Over the next few years, dozens of toll roads, called turnpikes, were built. (A pike, or pole, was placed across the road and raised when a traveler paid the toll, or usage fee.) The longest turnpike, the National Road, stretched from Cumberland, Maryland, west into Illinois. Even though roads were better than they had been in colonial times, the cost of shipping freight by road was much higher than by canal.

FULTON'S FOLLY

When Robert Fulton mounted a steam engine on a boat to power paddle wheels, people laughed at what they nicknamed "Fulton's Folly." But in 1807, his steamboat, the *Cleremont*, chugged up the Hudson River, against the forceful current, at a breathtakingly fast speed of five miles per hour. By 1830, steamboats churned up and down the major rivers and across the lakes of the United States. Like turnpikes and canals, steamboats were important to the rapid settling of the West. Settlers could travel upstream to lands beyond the Mississippi River, and ship farm products back to eastern cities.

The *Cleremont*.

41

TRAILS WEST

RUGGED PIONEERS OPEN UP NEW LANDS

Covered wagons near Scotts Bluff in
Nebraska along the Oregon Trail.

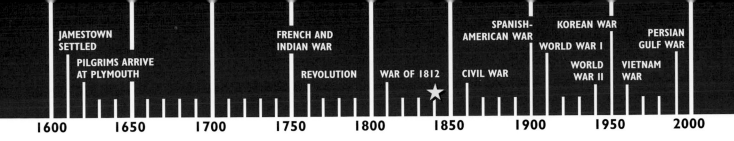

| JAMESTOWN SETTLED | | FRENCH AND INDIAN WAR | | | SPANISH-AMERICAN WAR | KOREAN WAR | PERSIAN GULF WAR |
| PILGRIMS ARRIVE AT PLYMOUTH | | | REVOLUTION | WAR OF 1812 | CIVIL WAR | WORLD WAR I | WORLD WAR II | VIETNAM WAR |

| 1600 | 1650 | 1700 | 1750 | 1800 | 1850 | 1900 | 1950 | 2000 |

- **1775** Daniel Boone opens the Wilderness Road into Kentucky
- **1803** The Louisiana Purchase adds more than 800,000 square miles of western lands
- **1821** The first American settlers are allowed in Mexican Texas
- **1841** The first wagon train heads to Oregon and California
- **1847** Mormons reach the Great Salt Lake

In some places in the West, you can still see deep wagon ruts made by pioneer wagon trains more than 150 years ago. Throughout the 1800s, rugged pioneers risked their lives to reach new lands and opportunities in the West.

By 1820, much of the region east of the Mississippi River had been settled. Land-hungry settlers headed 2,000 miles farther west, to Oregon and California. They skipped over the Great Plains, which were called the Great American Desert, because the land was too dry to farm and the prairie sod was too thick to plow. In 1841, the first wagon train headed out the Oregon Trail, across the prairie and through the Rocky Mountains. Within four years, 10,000 more wagon trains had made the dangerous six-month journey to Oregon Territory. Many people died along the way from disease, hunger, accidents, and attacks by Native Americans.

Smaller groups of pioneers branched off on the California Trail, through the Sierra Nevada into California. California had become a province of Mexico when the Mexicans won their independence from Spain in 1821. Mormons, a religious group, headed to the desert region of Utah after being persecuted in the East. They used irrigation to transform the region around the Great Salt Lake, founding prosperous farming settlements. Still other settlers went into another Mexican province—Texas.

A scene from the tragic Trail of Tears.

THE TRAIL OF TEARS

Land hunger blinded Americans to the rights of Native Americans. During the 1830s and 1840s, nearly all the southeastern tribes were forced to give up their lands to the United States. Even worse, more than 100,000 Native Americans were ordered to move to "Indian Territory" west of the Mississippi River. The Cherokees, who resisted, were forced to march 1,700 miles under army guard. An estimated 4,000 out of 15,000 died on this long, cruel journey, which became known as the "Trail of Tears."

MOUNTAIN MEN LEAD THE WAY

Long before pioneer wagon trains traveled through the snow-capped Rockies and Sierra Nevada, rugged fur-trappers known as "mountain men" explored the region. In their search for beaver pelts and other furs, they became the first easterners to penetrate the western mountains. The mountain men found the best passes through mountain barriers and often served as guides for both the wagon trains and the army.

WAR WITH MEXICO

AMERICA'S FIGHT FOR LAND IN THE WEST

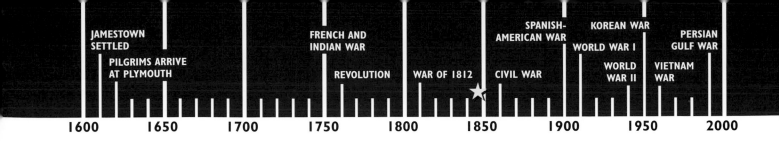

JAMESTOWN SETTLED			FRENCH AND INDIAN WAR			SPANISH- AMERICAN WAR	KOREAN WAR	PERSIAN GULF WAR
	PILGRIMS ARRIVE AT PLYMOUTH			REVOLUTION	WAR OF 1812	CIVIL WAR	WORLD WAR I	WORLD WAR II	VIETNAM WAR

1600   1650   1700   1750   1800   1850   1900   1950   2000

- 1836 The Alamo is stormed
    Texas declares its independence
    from Mexico
- 1845 Texas becomes the 28th state
- 1846 The United States declares war
    against Mexico
    Great Britain settles the Oregon
    boundary with the United States
- 1847 Mexico surrenders
- 1848 Mexico cedes California and the
    southwest region to the
    United States

As pioneers pushed westward, many Americans dreamed of seeing the nation expand from "sea to shining sea"—from the Atlantic Ocean to the Pacific. But the land west of the Rockies did not belong to the United States. Great Britain claimed much of the region called Oregon, and Mexico controlled California.

When James K. Polk was elected president in 1844, he was determined to realize the dream of expansion to the Pacific. First, Polk persuaded Great Britain to give up its claims in Oregon. Then, Texas, a former Mexican province, joined the Union, and relations with Mexico soured. When American and Mexican troops clashed near the Rio Grande, Polk asked Congress to declare war against Mexico.

As soon as the war with Mexico began in 1846, American settlers in California revolted against Mexican rule. They soon gained control of California and raised the flag of the Republic of California. Around the same time, American troops invaded Mexico by land and by sea. In 1847, Mexico City was captured, and the Mexican government asked for peace. In the 1848 peace treaty, Mexico gave up nearly half its territory, an area that included present-day California, New Mexico, Arizona, Utah, Nevada, and parts of Colorado and Wyoming.

◀ The Battle of Molino del Rey, in the war with Mexico.

TEXAS:
THE LONE STAR REPUBLIC

Beginning in the 1820s, Americans had been allowed to settle in the Mexican province of Texas if they declared loyalty to Mexico. But the settlers still thought of themselves as Americans, and in 1836, they declared independence. They formed an army, with Sam Houston in command. Despite several early losses, the Texan rebels won and established the Republic of Texas, or the Lone Star Republic. Texas remained an independent country until it was admitted into the United States in 1845.

THE ALAMO

In 1836, the ruler of Mexico, General Antonio López de Santa Anna, sent an estimated 5,000 troops into Texas to gain firmer control of the province. A band of about 190 Americans defied Santa Anna. They fortified themselves in a former mission (a religious community) called the Alamo. Although they were badly outnumbered, the Americans, including frontiersmen Davy Crockett and Jim Bowie, refused to surrender. For two weeks, Santa Anna's cannons bombarded the stronghold. On March 6, 1836, the Mexicans stormed the walls and killed all the defenders. The slogan "Remember the Alamo!" became the rallying cry of the Texans' fight for independence.

General Antonio López de Santa Anna of Mexico.

THE GOLD RUSH

WESTERN EXPANSION BOOMS

Gold-seekers pan for gold in California.

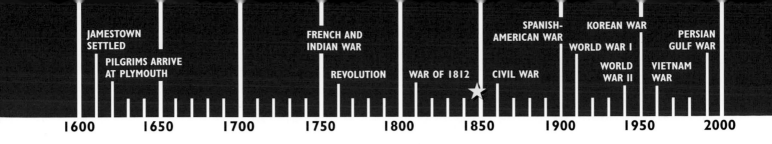

| JAMESTOWN SETTLED | | FRENCH AND INDIAN WAR | | | SPANISH-AMERICAN WAR | KOREAN WAR | PERSIAN GULF WAR |
| PILGRIMS ARRIVE AT PLYMOUTH | | REVOLUTION | WAR OF 1812 | CIVIL WAR | WORLD WAR I | WORLD WAR II | VIETNAM WAR |

1600   1650   1700   1750   1800   1850   1900   1950   2000

- **1848 Gold is discovered in California**
- **1849 Forty-Niners flood California**
- **1850 California becomes the 31st state**

On the morning of January 24, 1848, James W. Marshall was building a sawmill in northern California for his employer, John A. Sutter. When he saw yellow specks in the stream, he knew instantly what it was—gold. Although Sutter and Marshall tried to keep the discovery secret, word leaked out—there was gold in California!

"Gold fever" swept across the nation, and the gold rush was on. During 1849, about 100,000 people flocked to the California gold fields, putting up tent villages with names like Red Dog and Lazy Man's Camp. The rush of "Forty-Niners"—so named for the year—sent prices for basic items skyrocketing: $3 for an egg, $400 for a barrel of flour. The gold-seekers came from Mexico, Australia, Europe, and China, as well as the eastern United States.

Only a few of the Forty-Niners ever found the fortunes that lured them. Some, including Marshall and Sutter, ended up almost penniless. Others made fortunes by providing food, housing, and equipment to the miners. When the gold rush faded, California was transformed. In 1849, it had enough people to qualify as a territory. Just one year later, California was admitted to the Union.

An engraving of the American clipper ship *Flying Cloud*.

CALIFORNIA'S SPANISH HERITAGE

Spain claimed California in the 1500s, but two centuries passed before the Spanish began to settle it. The first settlements were a series of 22 Catholic missions

A Spanish mission in California.

(religious communities) built between San Diego and San Francisco. The missions became self-sustaining communities where the priests worked to convert Native Americans to Christianity and to a European way of life based on farming, herding, and crafts. For a time, 30,000 Native Americans lived in the mission communities. After declaring its independence from Spain in 1821, Mexico closed most of the missions and gave the land to settlers, who established large ranches. The Spanish influence in California can be seen today in the state's architecture, place names, and mixing of peoples.

CLIPPER SHIPS

Most Forty-Niners had to take the slow overland route to California, a journey that could take four months or more. Those who could afford it went by ship, often sailing around the tip of South America. The fastest ships in the world at that time were the American clipper ships, sleek vessels carrying acres of canvas sail. In 1851, the fastest clipper ship sailed from New York, around South America, to San Francisco in 89 days.

The Union Divided and Restored

*L*ike many Americans in the early 1800s, Thomas Jefferson worried that the question of slavery could tear the nation apart. The slavery issue, Jefferson wrote in 1820, was "like a firebell in the night [that] awakened and filled me with terror."

A Confederate soldier lies dead at Petersburg, Virginia, April 1865.

Although Americans were creating the world's most democratic nation, they had been unable to end slavery. The plantation economy of the South seemed to depend on slave labor. In the North, where slavery had been abolished by the 1820s, some people formed anti-slavery societies to work for emancipation—the freeing of all slaves. But most northerners did not feel strongly about the issue one way or the other.

As Americans moved west, between 1820 and 1860, the slavery issue went with them. Southerners insisted that slavery should be permitted in the new territories and states of the West; most northerners believed that the new lands should be free. When Abraham Lincoln was elected president in 1860, his Republican Party was opposed to slavery in the territories. Convinced that their entire way of life, including slavery, was threatened, 11 southern states decided to secede from, or leave, the United States. Their secession led to the Civil War. In this war, the North, or Union, was pitted against the South— named the Confederate States of America, often called simply the Confederacy.

At first it seemed as though the North would easily win the Civil War. By the 1860s, the northern states had a population of 22 million people. Only 9 million lived in the South, and nearly 4 million of this number were slaves. In addition, the North had three quarters of the nation's factories and railroads, so it had a great advantage in producing weapons, clothing, and other supplies. The southerners, however, were fighting on their home soil for a way of life they considered superior to the North's. The Confederacy also had talented military leaders.

The war raged from 1861 to 1865. It was the bloodiest war in the nation's history. At its end, the Union was restored, and slavery was abolished in all the states, North and South.

C H R O N O L O G Y

1837 Abolitionist Elijah P. Lovejoy is killed by a mob

1844 The first telegraph message is sent

1847 Frederick Douglass begins publishing the *North Star*

1850 The Fugitive Slave Act is passed

1852 *Uncle Tom's Cabin,* by Harriet Beecher Stowe, is published

1860 The Pony Express is formed

1861 The Civil War begins

Confederates win the First Battle of Bull Run

1862 The *Monitor* and the *Merrimack* battle

Confederates win the Second Battle of Bull Run

The Union wins the Battle of Antietam

Abraham Lincoln issues the Emancipation Proclamation

The Homestead Act offers settlers 160 acres of land for free

1863 The Battle of Gettysburg takes place

1865 General Robert E. Lee surrenders to General Ulysses S. Grant at Appomattox Court House

Abraham Lincoln is assassinated by John Wilkes Booth

The Thirteenth Amendment to the Constitution is ratified by the states, ending slavery forever

1867 William H. Seward arranges the Alaska Purchase

1869 The Union Pacific and Central Pacific Railroads meet in Utah

The U. S. government begins to place all Native Americans on reservations

1876 The Battle of the Little Bighorn is fought

1890 More than 200 Sioux die at Wounded Knee

THE UNDERGROUND RAILROAD

HELPING SLAVES TO FREEDOM

Escaped slave and publisher Frederick Douglass.

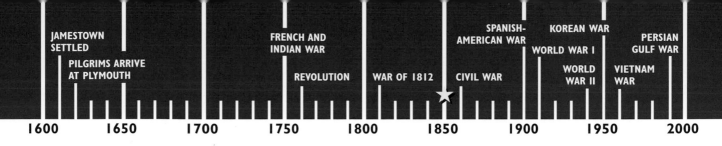

JAMESTOWN
SETTLED

PILGRIMS ARRIVE
AT PLYMOUTH

FRENCH AND
INDIAN WAR

REVOLUTION

WAR OF 1812

SPANISH-
AMERICAN WAR

CIVIL WAR

KOREAN WAR

WORLD WAR I

WORLD
WAR II

PERSIAN
GULF WAR

VIETNAM
WAR

1600   1650   1700   1750   1800   1850   1900   1950   2000

- 1832 The New England Anti-Slavery Society is formed
- 1837 Elijah P. Lovejoy is murdered in Illinois
- 1847 Frederick Douglass begins publishing the *North Star*
- 1850 The Fugitive Slave Act is passed
- 1852 *Uncle Tom's Cabin* is published

"We kept on our way on foot," Daniel Fisher, an escaped slave, recalled, "hiding by day and walking by night . . . with nothing to guide us but the North Star. . . . We were chased by men and hounds, but managed to escape capture, and finally arrived in Philadelphia." Fisher was one of thousands of slaves who escaped to freedom during the 30 years before the Civil War began. Whites and free African Americans guided the fugitives along carefully planned routes to the North or to Canada. This was the "Underground Railroad." Harriet Tubman, the most famous "conductor" on the Underground Railroad, herself escaped from slavery and then returned south 19 times, helping more than 300 slaves to freedom.

Men and women also formed organizations to fight slavery through meetings, speeches, and anti-slavery newspapers. Frederick Douglass, another escaped slave, started a newspaper, the *North Star*, and became a key figure in the New England Anti-Slavery Society. Many people in the North hated the abolitionists, as those who wanted to end slavery were called. Angry mobs sometimes wrecked the printing presses of anti-slavery newspapers or pelted the abolitionists with rocks. In 1837, a mob in Illinois attacked and killed Elijah P. Lovejoy, an abolitionist minister and newspaper publisher. But the fight against slavery could not be stopped.

THE FUGITIVE SLAVE ACT

When California applied for statehood in 1850, southerners were worried. California did not allow slavery, so if it joined the Union, there would be 17 free states and 16 slave states. The North would then be able to outvote the South in the U.S. Senate. Southern Senators would accept statehood for California only under certain conditions, including passage of a "fugitive slave" law, which would allow the capturing of escaped slaves anywhere in the nation. The Fugitive Slave Act was passed in 1850. Northerners were shocked when they saw African Americans being dragged through their streets in chains, to be returned south to slavery. The Fugitive Slave Act thus turned many people against slavery.

The Underground Railroad became increasingly important after the Fugitive Slave Act was passed.

UNCLE TOM'S CABIN

The anti-slavery movement gained still more strength in 1852, with the publication of Harriet Beecher Stowe's novel *Uncle Tom's Cabin*. The book, and stage plays based on it, provided vivid images of the cruelty of slavery. More than 300,000 copies of the book were sold within a year. Its dramatic story helped to convince many Americans that slavery must be ended.

THE CIVIL WAR BEGINS

A NATION DIVIDES AGAINST ITSELF

Stonewall Jackson at the Battle of Bull Run.

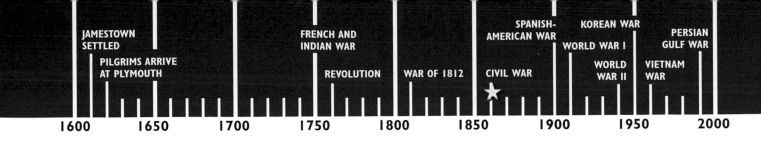

| JAMESTOWN SETTLED | | FRENCH AND INDIAN WAR | | | SPANISH-AMERICAN WAR | KOREAN WAR | | PERSIAN GULF WAR |
| PILGRIMS ARRIVE AT PLYMOUTH | | | REVOLUTION | WAR OF 1812 | CIVIL WAR | WORLD WAR I | WORLD WAR II | VIETNAM WAR |

1600   1650   1700   1750   1800   1850   1900   1950   2000

- **1861** On April 12, the Civil War begins
  The Confederates are victorious at Bull Run on July 21
- **1862** The *Merrimack* and *Monitor* battle to a draw
  General Ulysses S. Grant leads Union victories in the West
  General Robert E. Lee invades Maryland and threatens Washington, D.C.

When the Civil War began in April 1861, people on both sides thought that it would be a short, heroic war. An inkling of the long struggle ahead came a few months later, on July 21. A Union army marched south from Washington, D.C., and met a Confederate army near the town of Manassas Junction, Virginia, at a stream called Bull Run. When the southerners attacked, the Union soldiers panicked and ran, turning the battle into a lopsided and important victory for the South.

For the next year, Union forces tried repeatedly to take the Confederate capital, Richmond, Virginia. Each time, they were turned back by the "Rebels" under the brilliant leadership of Generals Robert E. Lee and Thomas "Stonewall" Jackson. Another Union force was attacking in the West, hoping to gain control of the Mississippi River. This western campaign produced a bold new leader—General Ulysses S. Grant. Grant led the Union to important victories on the Mississippi in 1862. Later that year, Lee took his army north into Maryland. His bold advance was to lead to a turning point in the war.

Stonewall Jackson

THE WAR AT SEA

After the war, Jefferson Davis, president of the Confederacy, said that one reason the South lost was that "we were without a navy while [the Union] had a powerful fleet."

Crewmen on the *Monitor*.

By building warships and arming merchant vessels, the North created a navy of 650 ships. This allowed it to blockade the South's coastline, cutting off badly needed supplies from England and other countries. The Confederates hoped that they could break the blockade with an iron-plated ship, the *Merrimack*, which they renamed the *Virginia*. But the Union Navy had its own "ironclad"—the *Monitor*. In March 1862, the first battle between ironclads ended in a draw, when the *Merrimack* was forced to withdraw, dashing the South's hope of destroying the blockade.

WOMEN AND MEDICAL CARE

Women played a key role for both sides in easing the suffering of the wounded and sick. Clara Barton, a former teacher, became known as the "Angel of the Battlefield" for her daring work near the front lines of the war. In Richmond, Sally Louisa Tompkins established one of the best hospitals in the Confederacy. Because medical science had not yet learned how germs spread disease, twice as many soldiers died of disease as of battle wounds. The women and men of the nursing services were constantly risking their lives in the fight against disease.

53

THE EMANCIPATION PROCLAMATION

PRESIDENT LINCOLN ENDS SLAVERY

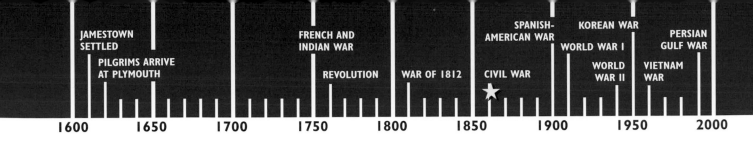

JAMESTOWN SETTLED		FRENCH AND INDIAN WAR			SPANISH-AMERICAN WAR	KOREAN WAR	PERSIAN GULF WAR
PILGRIMS ARRIVE AT PLYMOUTH		REVOLUTION	WAR OF 1812	CIVIL WAR	WORLD WAR I	WORLD WAR II	VIETNAM WAR

| 1600 | 1650 | 1700 | 1750 | 1800 | 1850 | 1900 | 1950 | 2000 |

• 1862 Confederates win the Second Battle of Bull Run

The Union wins a limited victory at Antietam

President Abraham Lincoln issues the Emancipation Proclamation

• 1863 The Emancipation Proclamation becomes law

At the start of the Civil War, President Abraham Lincoln said, "My paramount object in this struggle is to save the Union, and is not either to save or destroy slavery." Although many people urged him to issue a proclamation, or statement, setting the slaves free, he feared that doing so would lead the slave states still in the Union to join the Confederacy.

By 1862, however, Lincoln had come to believe that a proclamation of emancipation would help the Union cause. He wrote the statement that summer, but he waited until the Union won a battle to issue it, believing that a victory would make the statement stronger. That moment came at the Battle of Antietam, Maryland, in September 1862, when Union troops stopped General Robert E. Lee's Confederate advance into that state. Antietam was the bloodiest day of the war, with approximately 17,000 wounded and 6,000 killed. Five days later, on September 22, 1862, Lincoln issued his powerful and historic Emancipation Proclamation. The proclamation stated that on January 1, 1863, all slaves in the Confederacy would become "forever free."

Lincoln knew that this was a great moment for the nation. "If my name ever goes into history," he declared, "it will be for this act, and my whole soul is in it." From that moment on, Union soldiers were fighting for freedom as well as for national unity.

◄ President Abraham Lincoln.

The Battle of Antietam.

THE 54TH MASSACHUSETTS INFANTRY

Thousands of free African Americans served in the Union military during the Civil War. By 1865, about 186,000 had joined the army, and 30,000 more served in the navy. The most famous African-American unit was the 54th Massachusetts Infantry. The 54th fought with outstanding bravery in an assault on Fort Wagner in South Carolina, and went on to serve with distinction in other battles. Twenty-one African Americans were awarded the Congressional Medal of Honor for bravery.

THE THIRTEENTH AMENDMENT

Lincoln's proclamation was a war measure that declared free only the slaves in the Confederacy. He did this because he was not sure that the Constitution gave him the authority to free all slaves. To settle the question, the Thirteenth Amendment to the Constitution was passed by Congress and ratified by the states in 1865. In two simple sentences, the amendment forever ended slavery throughout the United States.

THE END OF THE CIVIL WAR

THE SURRENDER AT APPOMATTOX COURT HOUSE

Confederate general Robert E. Lee (center right) surrenders to
Union general Ulysses S. Grant (center left).

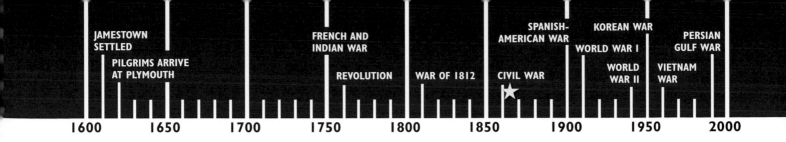

JAMESTOWN SETTLED

PILGRIMS ARRIVE AT PLYMOUTH

FRENCH AND INDIAN WAR

REVOLUTION

WAR OF 1812

CIVIL WAR

SPANISH-AMERICAN WAR

KOREAN WAR

WORLD WAR I

WORLD WAR II

VIETNAM WAR

PERSIAN GULF WAR

1600   1650   1700   1750   1800   1850   1900   1950   2000

- **1862 The Confederates are victorious at**
  Fredericksburg
- **1863 Confederate victory at Chancellorsville**
  The Battle of Gettysburg takes place
  President Abraham Lincoln delivers
  the Gettysburg Address
- **1865 General Robert E. Lee surrenders**
  at Appomattox Court House
  on April 9
  On April 14, Lincoln is shot

In June 1863, Confederate general Robert E. Lee decided to gamble everything on another invasion of the North. In the previous six months, his army had won two brilliant victories in Virginia. Lee hoped that another victory, this time on northern soil, would convince war-weary northerners to seek peace and recognize the Confederacy.

Lee's 75,000 men met a Union force of 90,000 at Gettysburg, Pennsylvania, on July 1, 1863. The Confederates hammered at the Union flanks for two days but could not break through. On the third day, a Virginia unit commanded by George E. Pickett led a Rebel assault on the Union center. After "Pickett's Charge" was slowed and then turned back by withering northern gunfire, Lee had no choice but to retreat into Virginia.

A few months later, Abraham Lincoln placed General Ulysses S. Grant, the hero of the Western battles, in command of all Union armies. Grant began a long, relentless pursuit of Lee. Tired, hungry, and low on supplies, the Confederates held out as long as they could. Finally, on April 9, 1865, Lee surrendered to Grant at Appomattox Court House, Virginia. The Civil War was over. The nation, however, had little time to celebrate: Just five days later, President Lincoln was killed.

THE GETTYSBURG ADDRESS

Four months after the Battle of Gettysburg, Lincoln traveled to the battlefield to help dedicate a battle cemetery. In his speech known as the Gettysburg Address, Lincoln helped Americans understand the meaning of the war: "We here highly resolve," the president said, "that these dead shall not have died in vain—that this nation, under God, shall have a new birth of freedom . . . . and that government of the people, by the people, for the people shall not perish from the earth."

THE ASSASSINATION OF PRESIDENT LINCOLN

On the night of April 14, 1865, President and Mrs. Lincoln attended a play at Ford's Theatre in Washington, D.C. John Wilkes Booth, an actor and a supporter of the Confederacy, entered the presidential box and shot the president. As Booth fled, Lincoln was carried to a nearby house, where he died the next morning. Booth was found in Virginia by Union troops and was killed. Lincoln's casket was carried on a 1,700-mile funeral journey through the country, as Americans mourned the passing of one of the nation's greatest presidents.

The funeral of President Lincoln.

THE TRANSCONTINENTAL RAILROAD

EAST MEETS WEST

The completion of the first transcontinental railroad,
in Promontory, Utah.

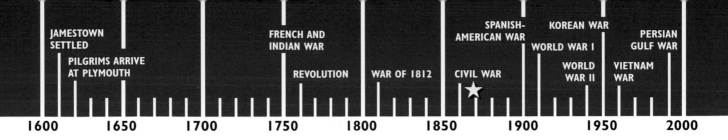

A rider for the Pony Express takes to the trail.

- 1844 The first telegraph message is sent
- 1860 The Pony Express is organized
- 1869 The Union Pacific and Central Pacific Railroads meet

In 1862, while the United States was deeply involved in the Civil War, Congress authorized two railroad companies to build a railroad that would link the East and West coasts of the United States for the first time. The Union Pacific Railroad began laying track westward from Omaha, Nebraska. The Central Pacific Railroad worked eastward from Sacramento, California.

The Union Pacific workers were mostly immigrants from Ireland. They endured brutal winter blizzards, broiling summer heat, and frequent attacks by Native Americans to lay some 1,700 miles of track across the vast prairie. The Central Pacific workers included more than 9,000 Chinese immigrants who bravely cut their way through the rugged Sierra Nevada Mountains.

Finally, in 1869, after six years of backbreaking work, the two lines met at Promontory Point, Utah Territory. A golden spike was driven into the last section of track to mark completion of the first transcontinental railroad.

Westward-bound wagon trains had once inched for four to six months across prairie and desert and through the mountains. Now the journey could be made in comfort in just a few days' time.

Over the next 30 years, four more extensive transcontinental lines were built. The railroad companies were given land along their routes, which they could then sell to settlers. The growth of the railroads thus encouraged thousands of people in the eastern United States and in Europe to join the westward movement.

THE PONY EXPRESS

In the mid-1800s, letters sent from the East to California might take two months or more to be delivered. In April 1860, the Pony Express was formed to speed communication. Daring young riders, taking turns on swift horses kept at relay stations, could carry mail between St. Joseph, Missouri, and San Francisco, California, in just 10 days. This was an amazing accomplishment, but the Pony Express existed for less than two years.

THE TELEGRAPH

The success of the Pony Express was ended by the telegraph, which had been invented by the artist and inventor Samuel F. B. Morse in the 1840s. Morse had developed a system for sending signals over electrical wires, using a dot-and-dash code system. For the first time in history, messages could be sent over long distances in a matter of minutes rather than days, weeks, or months. When telegraph lines were strung across the continent, there was no longer a need for the Pony Express.

Samuel Morse

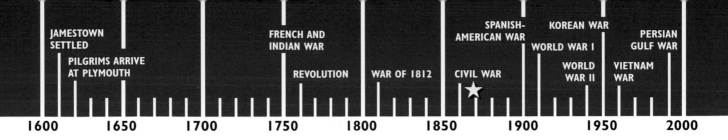

59

THE LAST FRONTIER

TAMING THE WILD WEST

During the second half of the eighteenth century, towns such as this were settled across the Western frontier.

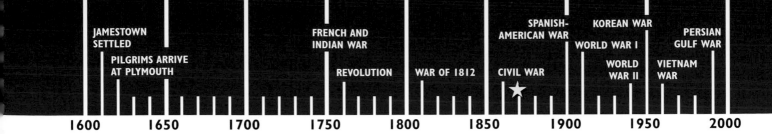

| JAMESTOWN SETTLED | | FRENCH AND INDIAN WAR | | | | SPANISH-AMERICAN WAR | KOREAN WAR | | PERSIAN GULF WAR |
| PILGRIMS ARRIVE AT PLYMOUTH | | | REVOLUTION | WAR OF 1812 | CIVIL WAR | | WORLD WAR I | WORLD WAR II | VIETNAM WAR |

| 1600 | 1650 | 1700 | 1750 | 1800 | 1850 | 1900 | 1950 | 2000 |

- **1851-1890 Thirteen new states are admitted**
- **1862 The Homestead Act encourages Western settlement**

Famed outlaw Jesse James.

In the closing decades of the nineteenth century, settlers headed west into the last open land—the Great Plains and the Rocky Mountains. This was the region that pioneers had passed over earlier in their push for Oregon and California. A new steel plow that could cut through the thick prairie sod helped farmers turn the Great Plains into seas of wheat and corn. Railroads sold land cheaply to attract settlers, and the Homestead Act gave families 160 acres free if they farmed it for five years.

The Rocky Mountain region became the nation's great mining frontier. Discoveries of gold, silver, copper, and other valuable metals peppered the Rockies with "boom towns" from Montana to Arizona. Many of these mining towns soon lost population and turned into "ghost towns." Others, like Denver, Colorado, grew to become major cities.

The popular heroes of the last frontier were the cowboys. From the mid-1860s to the 1880s, cowboys guided huge herds of longhorn cattle on long "drives" from Texas north, moving them to towns on the rail lines for shipment to meat-packing plants. But the days of the long cattle drives ended quickly. The invention of barbed wire led to the fencing in of more and more land. And severe blizzards in the late 1880s killed most of the open-range cattle. By 1890, cattlemen and cowboys worked on fenced ranches.

THE WILD WEST

During the 1870s and 1880s, eastern readers were fascinated by stories about the colorful characters of the mining camps and cattle towns of the West. They read about outlaws, such as Billy "the Kid" and Jesse James, and about lawmen, such as Wyatt Earp and "Wild Bill" Hickok, who helped bring order to some of the cattle towns. But the West was never as wild as the stories about it. "Buffalo Bill" Cody helped to create a romantic image of the West with his Wild West show, which toured the United States and Europe. Later, movies and television kept these legends alive.

THE PURCHASE OF ALASKA

People called it "Seward's Folly" and "Seward's Icebox," but Secretary of State William H. Seward went ahead with his plan anyway. In 1867, he arranged to purchase Alaska from Russia for $7.2 million; the treaty for the purchase was signed in 1884. Most Americans saw little value in what seemed to be a frozen wasteland. But a gold strike in 1896 provided a hint that Alaska was to be a great storehouse of natural resources—as well as America's last frontier.

Signing the treaty for the purchase of Alaska.

INDIAN WARS END

NATIVE AMERICANS ARE FORCED TO GIVE UP

The U.S. Cavalry charges into an Indian village.

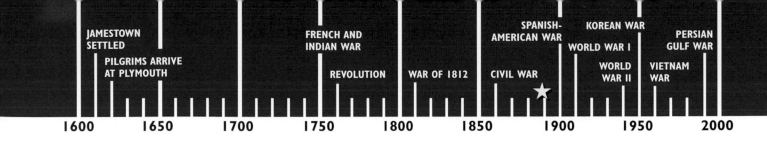

JAMESTOWN SETTLED		FRENCH AND INDIAN WAR			SPANISH-AMERICAN WAR	KOREAN WAR
PILGRIMS ARRIVE AT PLYMOUTH			WAR OF 1812		WORLD WAR I	PERSIAN GULF WAR
		REVOLUTION		CIVIL WAR	WORLD WAR II	VIETNAM WAR

1600   1650   1700   1750   1800   1850   1900   1950   2000

- **1869 The U.S. government starts a policy of placing all Native Americans on reservations**
- **1876 The Sioux are victorious at the Battle of the Little Bighorn**
- **1890 The Wounded Knee killings end armed resistance**

George Armstrong Custer.

As settlers, miners, and the railroads moved into the Great Plains, they touched off a series of bloody clashes with Native-American peoples, lasting from 1860 to 1890. Dozens of tribes, such as the Cheyenne and Sioux (Lakota), decided to fight rather than give up their lands and way of life.

The warfare was bitter and often cruel on both sides. In 1862, for example, Sioux warriors killed hundreds of men, women, and children in southern Minnesota. Two years later, a militia band raided a Cheyenne camp in Colorado, killing 450, mostly women and children. Gradually, however, cavalry units of the U.S. Army ended the Native-American resistance. By 1890, most Native Americans had been forced onto reservations—tracts of land set aside for them.

The last and one of the most tragic conflicts occurred that year in South Dakota. In December, an army regiment rounded up a band of 350 Sioux near Wounded Knee Creek in South Dakota. As soldiers were disarming the Sioux, a gun went off. The soldiers panicked and opened fire. More than 200 Sioux men, women, and children died in the gunfire.

THE BATTLE OF THE LITTLE BIGHORN

Colonel George Armstrong Custer, a man known to Native Americans as "Yellow Hair," confidently marched his troops toward a gathering of Sioux and Cheyenne in Montana Territory. It was June 1876, and back in Philadelphia, Americans were celebrating the nation's Centennial—the 100th anniversary of independence. With only about 265 of his men, Custer rode toward the Little Bighorn River, where he expected to surprise a few hundred warriors. Instead, his command was surrounded by more than 3,000 Sioux, who killed Custer and all his men. It was to be the last Native-American military victory.

BISON ON THE PLAINS

For generations, the bison, or buffalo, had provided Native Americans with not only meat but also hides for clothing and teepees. In the late 1800s, however, the great bison herds were vanishing, slaughtered by white hunters for sport, for their hides, and for food for the armies of railroad workers. By 1890, the magnificent, shaggy bison, which had once numbered in the millions, were nearly extinct.

Bison once flourished on the American Plains.

America as a World Leader

Wilbur Wright photographs his brother Orville's test flight in 1909.

When the inventor Thomas Alva Edison was growing up in the 1850s, he liked to watch the wagon trains roll past his Ohio home on their way west. At that time, America was a nation of farm towns and small cities. People heated their homes with wood stoves, used oil or gas lamps for light, and traveled by horse and buggy or steam railroad.

By the time of his death in 1931, at the age of 84, Edison had witnessed, and had been part of, one of the greatest periods of change in human history. He saw huge new industries come into being, producing steel, automobiles, radios, airplanes, and other products that had been unimaginable in 1850. Edison himself helped to harness electricity, providing electric lights and the power to run machines and household appliances.

America became a world leader in manufacturing. By 1920, for the first time, more Americans lived in cities and suburbs than in rural areas. And inventions such as the automobile and the telephone forever changed the way that Americans lived.

The same period also saw the United States emerge as a world power. In 1898, a brief war with Spain presented the nation with an overseas empire that included Puerto Rico, Guam, and the Philippines. In 1917, America entered World War I, which had started in Europe in 1914. When peace came in 1918, Americans hoped that this had been "the war to end all wars." Instead, in 1941, the threat created by dictators in Germany, Japan, and Italy plunged the United States into World War II (1939-1945). The nation emerged from that war as the world's leading military power and the nation that others looked to as the defender of freedom and democracy across the globe.

1869 Wyoming Territory gives women the right to vote

1872 Susan B. Anthony is arrested for voting

1876 Alexander Graham Bell invents the telephone

1877 Thomas Edison invents the phonograph

1879 Edison invents the lightbulb

1880 Immigrants begin to arrive in America by the millions

1886 The Statue of Liberty is dedicated

The American Federation of Labor is formed

1895 Edison shows the first moving picture

1898 The United States declares war on Spain

Hawaii becomes a U. S. territory

1903 Mother Jones leads 300 child workers on a protest march

Wilbur and Orville Wright complete the first airplane flight

1913 Henry Ford uses an assembly line to produce automobiles

1914 The Panama Canal opens

1917 The United States enters World War I

1919 The Eighteenth Amendment, prohibiting the production or sale of alcohol, is passed

1920 The Nineteenth Amendment gives the vote to women

1927 Charles A. Lindbergh flies nonstop across the Atlantic

1929 The stock market collapses

1933 Dust storms begin in the Great Plains

1941 Pearl Harbor is bombed; America enters World War II

1945 The United States drops atomic bombs on Hiroshima and Nagasaki; World War II ends

NEW IMMIGRATION

AMERICA'S SHORES TEEM WITH HOPEFUL ARRIVALS

The immigration registration room at Ellis Island.

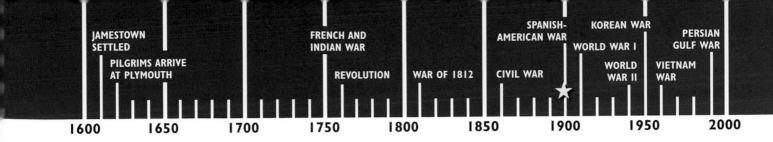

JAMESTOWN SETTLED

PILGRIMS ARRIVE AT PLYMOUTH

FRENCH AND INDIAN WAR

REVOLUTION

WAR OF 1812

CIVIL WAR

SPANISH-AMERICAN WAR

WORLD WAR I

KOREAN WAR

WORLD WAR II

VIETNAM WAR

PERSIAN GULF WAR

1600   1650   1700   1750   1800   1850   1900   1950   2000

- **1880-1920 Immigrants from Eastern and Southern Europe arrive in America by the millions**
- **1920s The United States sets new restrictions on immigration**

"Everyone was talking about going to America," a Polish girl wrote in 1897, "and we children played at being aboard ship, bound for 'the land of plenty.'" Millions of people in Europe and other parts of the world saw America as the land of hope and opportunity. Beginning in 1880, immigrants began arriving in greater numbers than ever before. Between 1880 and 1920, more than 23 million newcomers arrived.

Until this period, most immigrants had come from Western and Northern Europe—especially England, Ireland, Germany, and the Scandinavian countries, such as Sweden and Norway. After 1880, the "new immigration" brought large numbers from Eastern and Southern Europe—countries such as Russia, Poland, Italy, and Greece. Many of these newcomers encountered prejudice because they seemed "different"—they spoke a foreign language, and they were Catholics or Jews, which were both minority religious groups in America.

Most of the new immigrants headed for the cities, seeking factory jobs. They settled near others from the "old country," creating supportive ethnic neighborhoods. While life was often hard for the newcomers, their children and their children's children soon adopted American ways and blended into American society.

Many native-born Americans began to feel that too many immigrants were coming each year. In the 1920s, new laws reduced the flood of immigrants to a trickle, even though immigration had been a great source of the nation's strength.

THE STATUE OF LIBERTY

The Statue of Liberty.

"We stood on deck for hours," an Italian immigrant recalled, "peering through the fog for our first glimpse of the Statue of Liberty." For millions of immigrants, the Statue of Liberty was a symbol of what America stood for, and they eagerly looked for it as their ships approached New York Harbor. The statue, which stands 305 feet high with its pedestal, was a gift from the people of France, dedicated in 1886. At the base, a plaque is engraved with a poem by Emma Lazarus, expressing America's welcome to immigrants. It ends with the words, "I lift my lamp beside the golden door!"

ELLIS ISLAND

Dutch immigrant children at Ellis Island, c. 1906.

Many immigrants first set foot on American soil at Ellis Island, across the harbor from the Statue of Liberty. From 1892 to 1943, it was the main processing center for immigrants from Europe. Newcomers were given physical examinations, received their papers, and then took a ferry to the American mainland to begin their new lives. In 1965, Ellis Island was combined with the Statue of Liberty to form Liberty National Monument.

WORKERS DEMAND REFORM

SOCIAL POLICY BECOMES THE FOCUS

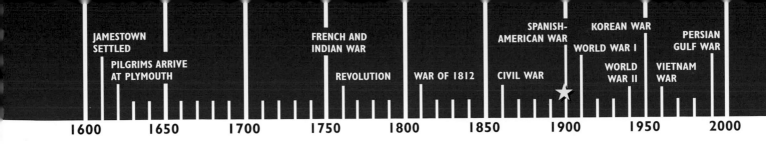

JAMESTOWN SETTLED			FRENCH AND INDIAN WAR			SPANISH-AMERICAN WAR	KOREAN WAR WORLD WAR I	PERSIAN GULF WAR
	PILGRIMS ARRIVE AT PLYMOUTH			REVOLUTION	WAR OF 1812	CIVIL WAR	WORLD WAR II	VIETNAM WAR

1600   1650   1700   1750   1800   1850   1900   1950   2000

- 1877 A labor strike cripples the eastern railroads
- 1886 The American Federation of Labor is formed
- 1894 Federal troops are called in to end a strike against the Pullman railroad-car company
- 1903 "Mother" Jones leads the March of the Mill Children
- 1935 New laws safeguard workers' right to form unions

"As a factory girl," a young woman wrote in 1898, "I am making $4.20 a week and spending $3 of this for board [room and meals] alone." Low wages were only one of the problems facing factory and mine workers in the late 1800s. They worked up to 14 hours a day. The work was dull and monotonous. Working conditions were unhealthy, and the machines caused frequent injuries. The sudden growth of new industries was creating an abundance of goods for many, and wealth for a few, but the workers and miners were suffering.

Change began when workers started organizing labor unions. Through a union, workers could demand better pay and improved working conditions. The unions' major weapon was the strike—workers refused work until their demands were met. The first strikes led to violence, when factory and mine owners, and the government, used force to "break" them. But the unions gradually won acceptance, and in the early 1900s, working conditions began to improve.

Men and women also began putting pressure on local, state, and national governments to pass laws to improve social conditions. This push for reform was called the Progressive Movement, and its followers became known as Progressives.

◀ A strike by New York garment workers.

Child workers at a Tennessee cotton mill.

ENDING CHILD LABOR

One of the worst abuses of the new industrial age was the widespread use of child workers. In 1900, nearly 2 million children under the age of 16 were working in factories and mines. They worked up to 13 hours a day for pay of about 60 cents. In 1903, a labor leader named Mary Harris "Mother" Jones led 300 child workers on a week-long march to President Theodore Roosevelt's home. This dramatic act helped convince people that child labor should be stopped.

IMPROVING CITIES

The sudden growth of cities in the late 1800s created problems—overcrowding, unsanitary conditions, crime, and poor services. The Progressives worked to correct these problems. Toledo, Ohio, led the way, under Mayor Samuel "Golden Rule" Jones. The city took control of such essential services as waterworks and electric plants. Toledo also showed other cities how to improve street lighting and police protection.

THE SPANISH-AMERICAN WAR AND NEW POSSESSIONS

Theodore Roosevelt as a Rough Rider in the Spanish-American War.

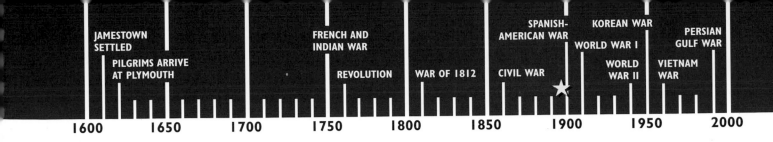

JAMESTOWN SETTLED

PILGRIMS ARRIVE AT PLYMOUTH

FRENCH AND INDIAN WAR

REVOLUTION

WAR OF 1812

CIVIL WAR

SPANISH-AMERICAN WAR

KOREAN WAR

WORLD WAR I

WORLD WAR II

VIETNAM WAR

PERSIAN GULF WAR

1600   1650   1700   1750   1800   1850   1900   1950   2000

- **1898** **The *Maine* explodes in Havana Harbor**
  The United States declares war
      against Spain
  An American fleet wins the Battle
      of Manila Bay
  On August 12, Spain surrenders
  In December, a peace treaty ends
      the war

On February 15, 1898, an explosion ripped through the U.S. battleship *Maine*, anchored off Havana, in Spanish Cuba. To this day, no one knows what caused the blast, which sank the ship. Americans, however, blamed Spain.

Relations between the two countries were already sour. Cubans were fighting for independence from Spain, and U.S. newspapers had whipped up anti-Spanish feeling with exaggerated reports of atrocities. Some Americans also believed that the United States should expand, perhaps by acquiring Cuba and other overseas territories. The sinking of the *Maine* brought matters to a head. Within months, the United States and Spain were at war.

Neither side was well prepared. But the American Navy defeated two Spanish fleets, one off Cuba and the other halfway around the world, in the Philippines. With no ships, the Spanish armies were cut off, and American ground forces were able to defeat them. The U.S. Army was helped by dozens of volunteer units. The most famous of these was the Rough Riders, led by Theodore Roosevelt. Roosevelt, who would later be president, led his unit on a famous charge at a site that came to be known as "San Juan Hill," near Santiago, Cuba.

The fighting lasted just four months. When it ended, Cuba gained independence. The United States gained control of several other Spanish possessions, including the Philippines and Puerto Rico.

THE ANNEXATION OF HAWAII

During the 1800s, American missionaries, sugar planters, and merchants became increasingly powerful in Hawaii. In 1893, the planters staged a successful revolt against Queen Liliuokalani, the Hawaiian ruler. They set up a government and asked the United States to annex the islands. During the Spanish-American War, the U.S. Congress agreed to annexation, and Hawaii became an American territory. Hawaii became a state in 1959.

THE PANAMA CANAL

For many years, Americans had been interested in building a canal across a narrow part of Central America. This would allow ships to move freely between the Atlantic and Pacific Oceans, without having to make the long, dangerous journey around the tip of South America. In 1903, the United States gained rights to a strip of land across the isthmus of Panama, and work on the canal was soon under way. Ten years later, in 1914, the Panama Canal opened, with the United States controlling the canal and a zone around it.

Construction of the Panama Canal.

NEW WAYS OF LIVING

MAJOR INVENTIONS CHANGE THE WORLD

A man displays an Edison phonograph.

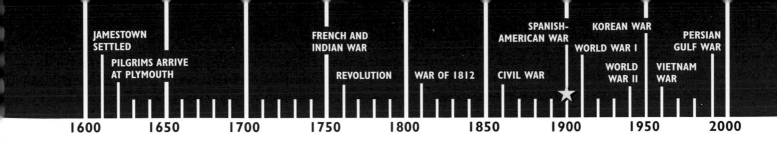

JAMESTOWN SETTLED		FRENCH AND INDIAN WAR				SPANISH-AMERICAN WAR	KOREAN WAR	PERSIAN GULF WAR
PILGRIMS ARRIVE AT PLYMOUTH		REVOLUTION	WAR OF 1812	CIVIL WAR		WORLD WAR I	WORLD WAR II	VIETNAM WAR

1600   1650   1700   1750   1800   1850   1900   1950   2000

- 1876 Alexander Graham Bell invents the telephone
- 1877 Thomas Edison invents the phonograph
- 1879 Edison invents the incandescent lightbulb
- 1903 The Wright brothers complete the first airplane flight
- 1913 Henry Ford produces the Model T
- 1920 The first commercial radio broadcast is aired

At the turn of the century, Americans were surrounded by startling new inventions, industries, and ideas. When Thomas Edison showed the first "moving picture" in 1895, police were needed to control the crowds who wanted to see the latest "miracle." Many of the new inventions, and the industries created from them, transformed the way Americans lived.

The automobile, for example, began as a curiosity in the 1890s, and then became a luxury for the wealthy. But in 1913, Henry Ford used a new assembly-line method to lower costs and mass-produce cars and trucks. By the mid-1920s, the old horse-drawn vehicles had been replaced by more than 20 million motor vehicles. The airplane, first demonstrated by Wilbur and Orville Wright in 1903, was another symbol of the new age. By 1930, some 38 airlines carried passengers to all parts of the country, and the first international flights had begun.

As electrical lines were stretched across the country, Americans not only enjoyed electric lights but also a host of new electrical appliances—refrigerators, vacuum cleaners, washing machines, and more. The telephone, invented in 1876, now provided instant communication in all but the most rural parts of the country. And with the introduction of radio broadcasts in 1920, people had access to news and information from all parts of the world.

Baseball fans crowd Ebbets Field in Brooklyn, New York.

THE AGE OF SPORTS

Until the late nineteenth century, most Americans had little free time for recreation. As living standards rose, and as machines and various household appliances replaced human labor, people had more leisure time, and a series of sports crazes swept the country. Outdoor activities such as bicycling, badminton, and croquet became popular. People took to baseball, football, and basketball, both as players and as spectators. Baseball was drawing 10 million fans a year by the 1920s, and in 1927, about 30 million people attended college football games. The 1920s also brought play-by-play radio broadcasts.

THE ENTERTAINMENT INDUSTRY

Thomas Edison developed the first crude phonograph in 1877 and the first motion pictures in 1895. The first movie with a story, *The Great Train Robbery*, was made in 1903. By the 1920s, both the recording and motion picture industries were providing entertainment for millions of people. By 1927, some 20,000 motion picture "palaces" were scattered throughout the country, and an estimated 100 million people went to the movies each week. At the time, the U.S. population numbered only about 123 million.

WORLD WAR I

THE FIRST MODERN WAR

A soldier, leaving to fight in the war, bids his family farewell.

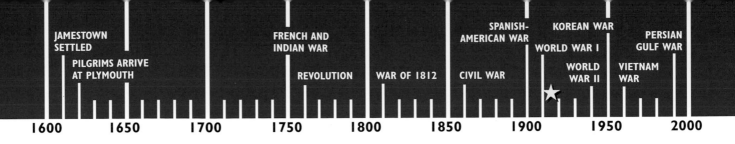

1600	1650	1700	1750	1800	1850	1900	1950	2000

JAMESTOWN SETTLED

PILGRIMS ARRIVE AT PLYMOUTH

FRENCH AND INDIAN WAR

REVOLUTION

WAR OF 1812

CIVIL WAR

SPANISH-AMERICAN WAR

KOREAN WAR

WORLD WAR I

WORLD WAR II

VIETNAM WAR

PERSIAN GULF WAR

- **1914** An assassination in Bosnia touches off World War I
  President Woodrow Wilson declares the United States neutral
- **1917** The United States enters the war
- **1918** An armistice ends the war
- **1920** The U.S. Senate rejects American membership in the League of Nations

"We crouched in our trenches," an American soldier wrote, "peering past the rolls of barbed wire and 'no man's land,' dreading the command that would send us 'over the top.'"

World War I, which began in Europe in August 1914, was the first war fought with modern weapons, such as tanks, machine guns, and submarines. The United States tried to remain neutral as the Central Powers, led by Germany, engaged in a deadly struggle against the Allied Powers, led by Great Britain and France. As both sides dug deep down in trenches along a 600-mile war front, the loss of life was devastating. In one battle that lasted six months, 650,000 men were killed or wounded—but only a few square miles of land changed hands.

The United States entered the war on the Allied side in 1917, partly because German submarines had preyed on American ships. Although Americans came late to the conflict, they played a key role. In the fall of 1918, more than a million American soldiers fought through the Argonne Forest in France for 47 days. The massive assault helped break the last German offensive. Germany finally agreed to an armistice on November 11, 1918. Hoping to avoid a future world war, the nations of the world formed the League of Nations in 1919. But the brutality of the war had convinced most Americans that it was best to stay out of "Europe's wars," and the United States refused to join the League.

THE WAR IN THE AIR

The most dashing heroes of the war were fighter pilots, daring aviators who wore leather jackets and flowing silk scarves. Less than a dozen years had passed since the Wright brothers' first flight, and the wooden, open-cockpit fighter planes were still primitive. Armed with machine guns, the planes engaged in spectacular "dog fights" in the skies over France. The top American "ace" was Lieutenant Eddie Rickenbacker, who shot down 26 enemy aircraft.

THE HOME FRONT

World War I was fought in Europe, but it still reached very deep into Americans' daily lives. Factories operated 24 hours a day. Daylight-savings time was introduced so that people could conserve electricity by not using their lights until later. Thousands of women found new jobs, working in factories, driving buses and taxicabs, performing office work for the army and navy, and serving in the nursing corps. One of the ideas the government used to boost people's patriotic spirit was to ask that the national anthem be sung at public events, a practice that continues today.

Women railroad workers during World War I.

75

VOTING RIGHTS FOR WOMEN

LANDMARK STEPS TOWARD EQUALITY

Women marching for suffrage, 1912.

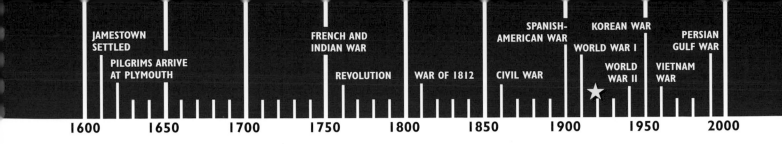

				SPANISH-	KOREAN WAR	
JAMESTOWN SETTLED		FRENCH AND INDIAN WAR		AMERICAN WAR	WORLD WAR I	PERSIAN GULF WAR
PILGRIMS ARRIVE AT PLYMOUTH		REVOLUTION	WAR OF 1812	CIVIL WAR	WORLD WAR II	VIETNAM WAR

1600   1650   1700   1750   1800   1850   1900   1950   2000

- **1848** **The Seneca Falls Convention takes place**
- **1869** **Women vote in Wyoming Territory**
  The National American Woman Suffrage Association is formed
- **1878** **A women's suffrage amendment is introduced in Congress**
- **1920** **The Nineteenth Amendment grants women the right to vote**

Women's suffrage buttons.

In 1873, Susan B. Anthony was arrested for the crime of casting a vote in the 1872 presidential election. Since women did not have suffrage—the right to vote—she had broken the law. Anthony was tried, found guilty, and fined $100. She refused to pay the fine and continued to work for women's voting rights until her death in 1906.

In the nineteenth century, most men—and many women—believed that government and politics were a "man's world." But women like Anthony defied their critics and carried on their voting rights crusade for 70 years. The major organization for their protests was the National American Woman Suffrage Association.

The first victories were won in the West. Wyoming Territory granted women the right to vote in 1869; with its statehood in 1890, Wyoming became the first state with women's suffrage. Slowly, other states followed suit. In 1919, Congress finally voted to send the Nineteenth Amendment to the states for ratification (approval). In 1920, the amendment, which is often called the Susan B. Anthony Amendment, was ratified in time for women to vote in the presidential election—almost a half-century after Anthony's protest vote.

THE SENECA FALLS CONVENTION

In 1848, three women—Elizabeth Cady Stanton, Lucretia Mott, and Martha Coffin Wright—organized a convention at Seneca Falls, New York. It was the first women's rights convention in the world. At the convention, Stanton read a "Declaration of Sentiment," based on the Declaration of Independence, asking that women be given full citizenship rights, including the right to vote. Most Americans at the time, however, considered the idea too radical to ever be taken seriously.

WOMEN AND THE ANTI-SLAVERY MOVEMENT

Many women, both white and African American, were active in the anti-slavery movement that began in the 1830s. When slaves were freed and gained their rights as citizens, they argued that those same rights should be extended to women. After the Civil War, the Fourteenth Amendment was passed, which guaranteed voting rights for African-American men. Leaders of the women's suffrage movement were extremely disappointed that they could not persuade Congress to include women in the amendment.

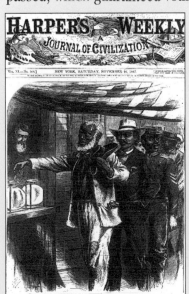

African Americans cast their votes for the first time in history.

77

THE ROARING TWENTIES

AMERICA'S GOLDEN DECADE

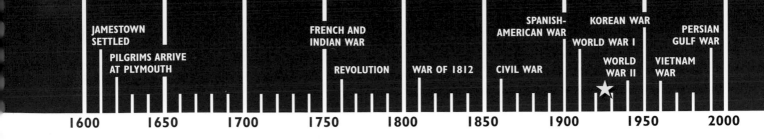

			SPANISH-AMERICAN WAR	KOREAN WAR	
JAMESTOWN SETTLED		FRENCH AND INDIAN WAR		WORLD WAR I	PERSIAN GULF WAR
PILGRIMS ARRIVE AT PLYMOUTH		REVOLUTION	WAR OF 1812	CIVIL WAR	WORLD WAR II	VIETNAM WAR

1600   1650   1700   1750   1800   1850   1900   1950   2000

- **1927 Charles Lindbergh makes the first nonstop, solo transatlantic flight**
  Mount Rushmore is dedicated
  Babe Ruth hits his 60th home run
  Heavyweight boxing champion Gene Tunney defeats Jack Dempsey
  ***The Jazz Singer* is the first motion picture with sound**

Prohibition did not stop drinking; a bar scene in the 1920s.

In 1928, presidential candidate Herbert Hoover declared that "We in America are [close to] the final triumph over poverty." To many Americans, the 1920s did indeed seem to be a golden decade. Factories were turning out record amounts of new products—automobiles, radios, refrigerators, and luxury items. Many people were making fortunes by investing in the stock market.

The decade has been labeled "the Jazz Age," for the music craze that swept the country. Jazz was the latest African-American contribution to music, building on earlier styles of gospel music, ragtime, and the blues.

This was also the decade when the nation tried "the noble experiment" of Prohibition—the outlawing

◄ Detroit police display an illegal liquor-manufacturing operation.

of all alcohol production and sales. The Eighteenth Amendment, banning alcohol, was approved in 1919. Behind the measure was the hope that it would improve society. But Prohibition failed from the start. People went to illegal "speakeasies" to drink, and they bought "bootleg" liquor. Gangsters like Al Capone took over the illegal alcohol business and engaged in a continuous violent battle with police, the Federal Bureau of Investigation, and others.

Quick fortunes and fast living gave the decade its best-known name—the "Roaring Twenties." But the good times came to a sudden stop when the stock market collapsed in October 1929. The nation then entered the worst economic depression in its history.

SHEIKS AND FLAPPERS
Young people of the 1920s wanted to rebel against tradition. Young men drove fast cars, wore raccoon-fur coats, and slicked down their hair to look like movie star Rudolph Valentino in *The Sheik*. Young women wore short hair, short dresses, rolled-down stockings, and lots of bead necklaces. These flappers, as they were called, broke sharply with the conventions of the day and led free-spirited lives.

AN AGE OF HEROES
Never before had Americans had so many colorful heroes. A shy, handsome aviator—Charles A. Lindbergh—became the greatest hero of the age in 1927, when he made the first nonstop solo flight across the Atlantic Ocean. Baseball player Babe Ruth was the towering figure among dozens of sports heroes. And movies, both silents and "talkies," produced a galaxy of Hollywood stars.

79

THE GREAT DEPRESSION

THE STOCK MARKET CRASH AND ECONOMIC RUIN

A soup kitchen during the Great Depression.

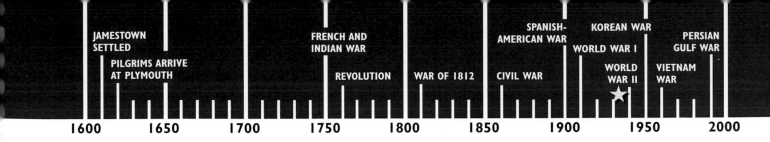
- 1929 The stock market crashes
- 1932 Franklin D. Roosevelt is elected president
- 1933 Roosevelt's New Deal offers economic relief
- 1936 Roosevelt wins re-election as president; re-elected in 1940 and 1944, FDR becomes the first president to serve more than two terms

In the "crash" of October 1929, the price of stocks, which represent ownership shares in corporations, fell so low that many became worthless. Millions of people lost the money that they had invested. In the months that followed, corporations laid off workers or went bankrupt. Banks ran out of money and closed their doors. This was the start of the Great Depression.

By the early 1930s, some 13 million people were out of work—more than half the workforce in some cities. There were no government programs to help, and churches and private charities soon ran out of funds. Men sold apples on street corners. Others went door to door, asking for odd jobs or handouts of food, and still others "rode the rails" of the freight trains, searching for work. Long lines formed outside community "soup kitchens."

In 1933, Franklin Delano Roosevelt, known as "FDR," became president and promised "a new Deal for the American people." This New Deal consisted of dozens of government programs to provide economic relief and long-term security. Many programs that help people today were started in the New Deal, including Social Security, unemployment insurance, and aid for the disabled. The Great Depression lingered through the 1930s. The New Deal did not solve all the country's problems, but it helped restore people's confidence and established the idea that the government should help people in times of emergency.

An Oklahoma dust storm.

THE DUST BOWL

One farmer said that the dust storms that swept across the Great Plains were "like a wall of dirt— fences, machinery, crops, and trees were gone, buried." From 1933 to 1937, such violent storms scoured the soil from North Dakota to Texas. Years of overfarming the land had loosened the topsoil. When a prolonged drought struck, the soil simply turned to dust and was carried off by the hot, dry winds. Thousands of families lost everything and became migrants, heading west in search of work. Some 30,000 families moved to farm camps in California.

FIRST LADY ELEANOR ROOSEVELT

Shy and unsure of herself, Eleanor Roosevelt knew that she faced a difficult challenge when her husband, Franklin, was paralyzed by polio in 1921. She not only had to raise their five children but also act as FDR's "eyes and ears" so that he could continue his political career. Before and after his election to the presidency, she traveled extensively, delivered thousands of speeches, and gathered information. One of her favorite accomplishments as First Lady was convincing FDR to place more African Americans in government positions than had all previous presidential administrations combined.

81

THE AXIS POWERS AGAINST THE ALLIES

Patriotic advertising in World War II.

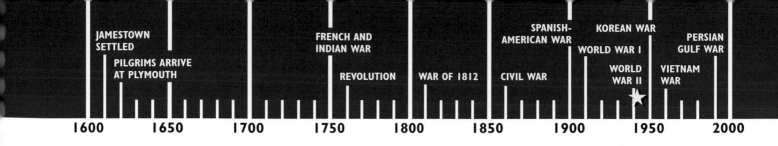

JAMESTOWN SETTLED

PILGRIMS ARRIVE AT PLYMOUTH

FRENCH AND INDIAN WAR

REVOLUTION

WAR OF 1812

SPANISH-AMERICAN WAR

CIVIL WAR

KOREAN WAR

WORLD WAR I

WORLD WAR II

PERSIAN GULF WAR

VIETNAM WAR

1600   1650   1700   1750   1800   1850   1900   1950   2000

- **1939 Nazi Germany invades Poland**
  Britain and France declare war
  against Germany
- **1941 Japan attacks Pearl Harbor**
  The United States enters the war
- **1944 June 6 is D-Day**
- **1945 Franklin D. Roosevelt dies; Harry S.**
  Truman becomes president
  Germany surrenders on May 7
  After atomic bombs destroy
  Hiroshima and Nagasaki, Japan
  surrenders on September 2

On December 7, 1941, a quiet Sunday was shattered by a shocking radio bulletin: The Japanese had attacked America's Pearl Harbor naval base at Honolulu, Hawaii. The surprise attack plunged the United States into World War II (1939-1945), the most destructive war in human history.

The war had been started by dictators obsessed with conquest. Japan had taken over much of Asia and the Pacific. Germany, led by the Nazi dictator Adolf Hitler, had conquered much of Europe. Civilians as well as soldiers were casualties of this war. Hitler, who was determined to create "racial purity," had millions of people murdered in Nazi "death camps," including 6 million Jews.

The American people rallied behind an all-out war effort. The production of peacetime goods such as automobiles was halted. Factories now turned out bombers, fighter planes, and ships. Nearly 13 million men and women served in the U.S. military. Children helped by planting "victory gardens" and collecting scrap metal and paper. Slowly, the United States and its allies turned the tide, liberated the conquered lands, and destroyed the dictatorships. At the war's end, the United States led the way in creating the United Nations, fashioned from the earlier League of Nations, to help preserve peace.

D-DAY

In the predawn hours of June 6, 1944, the largest invasion force in history left England, crossed the English Channel, and landed troops on the beaches of Normandy, France. This was D-Day—the Allied invasion of France to liberate Europe from German occupation. In the weeks that followed, against fierce German opposition, the Allied forces pushed inland. Meanwhile, troops from the Soviet Union struck at Germany from the east. The following spring, as the Allies closed in from both sides, Adolf Hitler committed suicide, and Germany finally surrendered.

American troops land on the coast of France on D-Day, 1944.

THE WAR IN THE PACIFIC

While engaged in the desperate struggle in Europe, Americans and their allies were also fighting the Japanese halfway around the world, in the islands of the Pacific Ocean. One island after another was invaded and the Japanese defenders killed or captured. As the Allies neared the islands of Japan itself, the decision was made to use the world's first atomic bombs to hasten the end of the war. After bombs destroyed the cities of Hiroshima and Nagasaki, Japan surrendered on September 2, 1945. A war that had claimed an estimated 55 million lives was finally over.

THE NUCLEAR AGE DAWNS

NEW WEAPONS OF UNPRECEDENTED POWER

An atomic bomb is tested at Eniwetok Atoll, 1948.

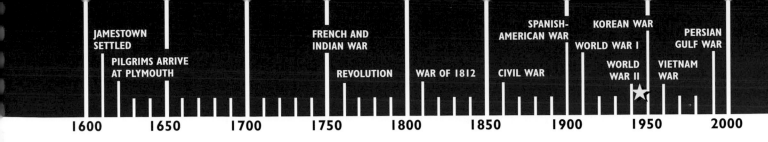

JAMESTOWN SETTLED
PILGRIMS ARRIVE AT PLYMOUTH
FRENCH AND INDIAN WAR
REVOLUTION
WAR OF 1812
CIVIL WAR
SPANISH-AMERICAN WAR
KOREAN WAR
WORLD WAR I
WORLD WAR II
VIETNAM WAR
PERSIAN GULF WAR

1600   1650   1700   1750   1800   1850   1900   1950   2000

- 1942 The Manhattan Project is launched
- 1945 The first test of an atomic explosion occurs in New Mexico
  In August, atomic bombs are dropped on Hiroshima and Nagasaki
- 1954 The first atomic power plant is built to produce electricity

In 1939, when World War II broke out in Europe, a group of scientists warned President Franklin D. Roosevelt that Nazi Germany was developing a

Physicist Enrico Fermi.

powerful new weapon: an atomic bomb, which would explode with incredible force created by splitting atoms. The scientists urged the president to start an American program to build such a bomb before the Germans succeeded in doing so.

In 1942, after the United States entered the war, Roosevelt established a top-secret program, giving it the code name "Manhattan Project." More than 125,000 people worked to develop the bomb, led by scientists such as Enrico Fermi and J. Robert Oppenheimer. The first test device was exploded in

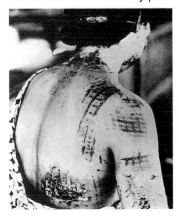

An atomic bomb victim in Japan.

the New Mexico desert on July 16, 1945. President Roosevelt had died a few months earlier, and Germany had surrendered. It was up to President Harry S. Truman to decide whether to use the new weapon against Japan. Truman believed that it would end the war quickly, saving lives that would be lost if the Allies had to invade Japan. A warning was sent to the Japanese government. When no reply was received, an atomic bomb was dropped on the city of Hiroshima on August 6, 1945. A second bomb was dropped on Nagasaki three days later. The explosions leveled the cities, claiming at least 200,000 lives and forcing Japan to surrender.

NUCLEAR ENERGY

In the years following World War II, many scientists believed that nuclear energy—energy released by splitting the nucleus, or center, of an atom—would supply the nation with an abundant supply of safe and cheap electrical power. The first nuclear power plant was built near Pittsburgh, Pennsylvania, in 1954, and dozens more were built or planned over the next 20 years. But problems developed. The plants were costly to build, and no safe way was found to dispose of their radioactive wastes. Several accidents also made people aware of the dangers of nuclear energy. Although nuclear power plants continued to supply about 15 percent of the nation's electricity in the 1990s, no new plants were scheduled to be built.

THE NUCLEAR ARMS RACE

From the 1950s through the 1980s, the two world "superpowers"—the United States and the Soviet Union—engaged in a costly and frightening nuclear arms race. Together, these two powers developed enough nuclear weapons to destroy civilization many times over. In the early 1990s, the final collapse of communism in the Soviet Union and Eastern Europe helped to ease the crisis, but by then, several other countries had developed nuclear weapons.

85

New Challenges

*A*merica emerged from World War II as the world's wealthiest and most powerful nation. For three decades after the war, Americans enjoyed a prosperity that was a model for the world. Not only was their standard of living higher than it ever had been before, but the United States also had the resources to help the war-torn countries recover, including the defeated enemies.

Building the Berlin Wall.

The prosperous years at home were clouded by a costly rivalry with the Communist Soviet Union, the world's other superpower. As the Soviets worked to spread communism, the United States worked to halt its spread. The icy relations between the two superpowers produced the Cold War— "cold" because they did not actually fight a war. But opposition to communism led the nation into several small armed conflicts and two major ones—the Korean War and the Vietnam War. The Vietnam conflict deeply divided the American people, cost 58,000 American lives, and contributed to an enormous national debt.

At home, African Americans led the way in a civil rights movement that hammered away at the walls of segregation, discrimination, and prejudice. Great progress was made in achieving more equal opportunity and greater political participation for members of minority population groups and for women.

In their eagerness to produce more and more goods, Americans often paid little attention to the ways in which they were harming the environment. Then, in 1962, the marine biologist Rachel Carson wrote a book entitled *Silent Spring*. That book and other warnings helped awaken Americans to the ways in which they were polluting the air, water, and land, and an environmental movement emerged. Since then, the government and the people have become more responsible about protecting the natural environment and conserving its limited resources. But as the nation approaches the twenty-first century, Americans realize that much more remains to be done to achieve these important goals.

C H R O N O L O G Y

1946 The "baby boom" begins as veterans of World War II come home

      The first electronic computer is created

1950 The Korean War begins

1953 Dr. Jonas Salk announces the creation of the polio vaccine

1954 The U.S. Supreme Court declares segregated schools unconstitutional

1955 Rosa Parks is arrested for refusing to give up her seat on a bus to a white man

1956 The U.S. government launches the interstate highway system

1957 The Soviet Union launches *Sputnik I*

1960s The United States becomes involved in the war in Vietnam

1961 The Berlin Wall divides Berlin, Germany, into east and west

1962 Rachel Carson's *Silent Spring* is published

      The Cuban Missile Crisis takes place

1963 More than 200,000 civil rights supporters march in Washington, D. C.

      John F. Kennedy is assassinated

1968 Martin Luther King, Jr., is assassinated

      Robert F. Kennedy is assassinated

1969 *Apollo 11* lands on the moon

1973 U.S. combat troops leave South Vietnam

      Richard M. Nixon becomes the first U.S. president to resign

1986 The space shuttle *Challenger* explodes after liftoff from Cape Canaveral

1991 The Persian Gulf War is fought

THE 1950s

POSTWAR PEACE AND PROSPERITY

U.S. Interstate Highway 80.

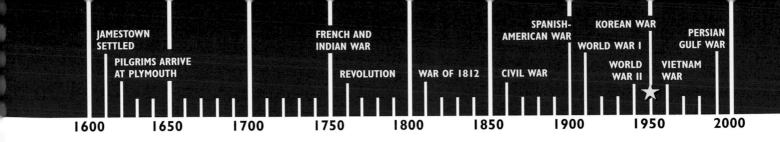

JAMESTOWN SETTLED		FRENCH AND INDIAN WAR			SPANISH-AMERICAN WAR	KOREAN WAR		PERSIAN GULF WAR
PILGRIMS ARRIVE AT PLYMOUTH						WORLD WAR I		
			REVOLUTION	WAR OF 1812	CIVIL WAR		WORLD WAR II	VIETNAM WAR

1600   1650   1700   1750   1800   1850   1900   1950   2000

- **1944 The GI Bill helps veterans buy homes and go to college**
- **1953   A polio vaccine is found**
- **1955 "Rock Around the Clock" becomes the first rock-and-roll hit**
- **1956 An interstate highway system is started**

After the troubles of the Great Depression and World War II, Americans could hardly wait to get back to the quiet routines of daily life. The decade of the 1950s was a time of peace and prosperity that allowed them to do just that. But daily life in America also changed in important ways.

Under the GI Bill, war veterans were given financial help in attending school and buying homes. Many married and began to raise families. From 1946 to the late 1950s, the birth rate jumped in what became known as the "baby boom." Young families moved in growing numbers from cities to suburbs, where housing developments and shopping centers were rapidly springing up. With people living farther from their jobs, the automobile became more important than ever. To handle the growing traffic, the government launched the interstate highway system in 1956. It now includes more than 40,000 miles of highway nationwide.

Every home seemed to sprout a television antenna, as the number of television sets soared from 1 million to 50 million by the end of the decade. The children of the 1950s, the "baby boomers," were the first generation to grow up with this exciting new form of entertainment. As they grew older, they would have a powerful influence on American styles and tastes.

A housing development in Levittown, New York.

Bill Haley and the Comets.

ROCK-AND-ROLL

For a decade after 1945, the most popular music was "mood music"—soft songs crooned by singers like Dinah Shore and Tony Bennett. Then, in 1955, a new sound exploded on the scene, when Bill Haley and the Comets recorded "Rock Around the Clock." Rock-and-roll really took off when a young singer named Elvis Presley made his first hit record. Although parents objected to the new sound, rock-and-roll quickly became the music of America's young.

MEDICAL MIRACLES

One of the most feared diseases before the 1950s was polio, or infantile paralysis. The virus struck mainly in the summer, and most of its victims were children. No one knew how the disease was spread. During epidemic years, public swimming pools and playgrounds were closed. In 1952, more than 57,000 people were stricken, and 3,300 died. One year later, Dr. Jonas Salk announced the development of a polio vaccine. The victory over polio is just one of many important achievements of medical science since 1950.

THE COLD WAR

TENSION BETWEEN THE WORLD'S TWO SUPERPOWERS

President John F. Kennedy at the Berlin Wall in 1963.

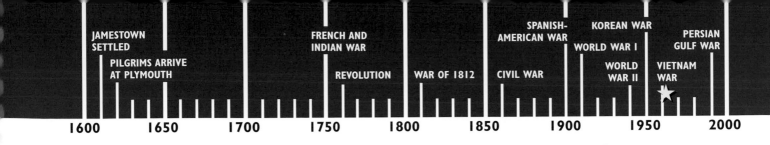

| JAMESTOWN SETTLED | | FRENCH AND INDIAN WAR | | | | SPANISH-AMERICAN WAR | KOREAN WAR | PERSIAN GULF WAR |
PILGRIMS ARRIVE AT PLYMOUTH · REVOLUTION · WAR OF 1812 · CIVIL WAR · WORLD WAR I · WORLD WAR II · VIETNAM WAR

1600   1650   1700   1750   1800   1850   1900   1950   2000

- **1950-1953 The Korean War is fought**
- **1961 The Berlin Wall divides East Berlin and West Berlin**
- **1960s-1970s The Vietnam War divides Americans**
- **1989-1991 Communism collapses in Eastern Europe and the Soviet Union**

"Cold War" was the term used to describe the hostility and tension that developed after World War II between the two "superpowers"—the United States and the Soviet Union. Following the world war, the Soviets had set up Communist governments in Eastern Europe and East Germany, where the divided city of Berlin became a symbol of the Cold War. In 1961, Communist leaders built a wall through the middle of the city, to prevent escape from the Communist zone. Communists also came to power in China, North Vietnam, North Korea, and Cuba.

From the late 1940s to the late 1980s, the United States followed a policy of containment—keeping communism from expanding. It sent military and economic aid to any country that was resisting communism. Billions of dollars were spent each year to strengthen the nation's military forces and to add to the arsenal of nuclear weapons. In 1962, the superpowers came to the very brink of war, when the Soviet Union began building nuclear missile sites in Cuba. Under President John F. Kennedy, the United States forced the Soviets to dismantle the sites, and this "Cuban Missile Crisis" ended peacefully.

Every American president in office after World War II searched for ways to ease tensions. But the Cold War did not really end until between 1989 and 1991, when the people of Eastern Europe rejected communism and the Soviet Union broke apart.

A South Korean child after the invasion of Inchon.

THE KOREAN WAR

Few Americans could have located Korea on a map before June 25, 1950, when Communist North Korea invaded South Korea. Less than five years after the end of World War II, American soldiers were again fighting on a distant battlefield, this time as part of a United Nations (UN) force. The Korean War lasted three years. At first, UN forces pushed deep into North Korean territory. But they were forced back when China entered the war on the North Korean side. President Harry S. Truman decided not to attack China itself, fearing that this would trigger a new world war. In July 1953, the two sides agreed to a truce. The border between North and South Korea remained unchanged.

THE SCIENCE AND TECHNOLOGY RACE

At the start of the Cold War, American scientists were well ahead of the Soviets in developing new, more powerful nuclear weapons and in other areas of military technology—missiles and electronics, for example. But the Soviets quickly caught up. In October 1957, the Soviet Union launched *Sputnik I*, the first artificial satellite to orbit the Earth. Americans feared that the Soviets would control space. The shock of the *Sputnik* launch led America to start a major effort in space exploration.

THE CIVIL RIGHTS MOVEMENT

THE COURAGEOUS STRUGGLE FOR EQUALITY

A view of the Washington Mall during the March on Washington.

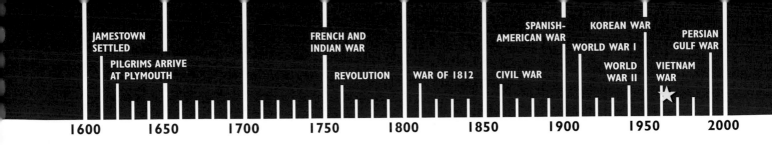

| JAMESTOWN SETTLED | FRENCH AND INDIAN WAR | | SPANISH-AMERICAN WAR | KOREAN WAR | PERSIAN GULF WAR |
| PILGRIMS ARRIVE AT PLYMOUTH | REVOLUTION | WAR OF 1812 | CIVIL WAR | WORLD WAR I WORLD WAR II | VIETNAM WAR |

1600   1650   1700   1750   1800   1850   1900   1950   2000

- **1954** The Supreme Court finds segregated schools unconstitutional
- **1955** The Montgomery bus boycott ends segregation in public transportation
- **1963** The March on Washington draws more than 200,000 civil rights supporters
- **1964** Congress passes sweeping civil rights legislation

"For Whites Only!" Signs with those words existed throughout the South as part of a policy of segregation—forcing African Americans to remain separate from whites. African Americans lived in segregated neighborhoods, went to separate and poorly funded public schools, and sat in separate areas on buses and theaters.

In the early 1950s, African Americans began to challenge segregation. In a landmark case, *Brown v. Board of Education of Topeka*, the Supreme Court found that the segregation of schools violated the Constitution.

Then, in December 1955, Rosa Parks was arrested in Montgomery, Alabama, for refusing to give up her bus seat to a white man. Led by a young preacher, Dr. Martin Luther King, Jr., African Americans protested by boycotting (refusing to ride) Montgomery buses. They won a court ruling declaring segregated seating to be illegal.

With the support of sympathetic white people, African Americans conducted one peaceful protest after another. They were often attacked and beaten by police and angry mobs, but they refused to resort to violence. More and more people began to support the demands for fairness and greater equality. Congress passed new civil rights laws to promote equality for all nonwhite Americans. Although prejudice and discrimination remained, Americans realized that they were making progress.

Martin Luther King, Jr., shakes hands after his "I Have a Dream" speech, 1963.

MARTIN LUTHER KING, JR.

In the most famous speech of the civil rights movement, the Reverend Martin Luther King, Jr., spoke to more than 200,000 people from the steps of the Lincoln Memorial in Washington, D.C., in 1963. "I have a dream," King declared, "that my four little children will one day live in a nation where they will not be judged by the color of their skin but by the content of their character." From 1955 to 1968, King led the movement, inspiring people with his words and actions, and always urging nonviolence. But King himself was the victim of violence: He was assassinated in April 1968.

THE SPREAD OF THE MOVEMENT

Other minority groups, such as Latinos, Asian Americans, and Native Americans, were inspired by the protests of African Americans. They, too, organized peaceful demonstrations for civil rights. These groups also made progress. Native Americans, for example, have gained control of the natural resources on their reservations and have established profitable businesses. Women, too, became part of the movement and opened new opportunities in business, government, education, and sports.

EXPLORATION OF SPACE

CONQUERING A BOLD NEW FRONTIER

Astronaut Buzz Aldrin on the moon.

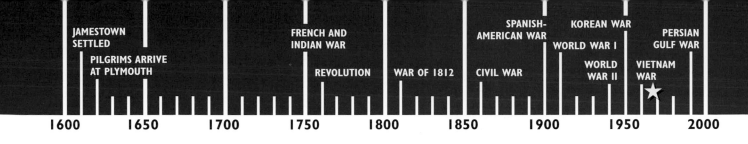

| JAMESTOWN SETTLED | | FRENCH AND INDIAN WAR | | | SPANISH-AMERICAN WAR | KOREAN WAR | PERSIAN GULF WAR |
| PILGRIMS ARRIVE AT PLYMOUTH | | | REVOLUTION | WAR OF 1812 | CIVIL WAR | WORLD WAR I | WORLD WAR II | VIETNAM WAR |

| 1600 | 1650 | 1700 | 1750 | 1800 | 1850 | 1900 | 1950 | 2000 |

- **1961** Astronaut Alan Shepard makes the first manned American space flight
- **1962** John Glenn, Jr., is the first American to orbit the Earth
- **1969** *Apollo 11* begins an eight-day journey to the moon
- **1986** The *Challenger* space shuttle explodes

"The Eagle has landed," astronaut Neil Armstrong calmly reported as he guided the lunar landing craft onto the surface of the moon. The date was July 20, 1969, and nearly 1 billion people worldwide watched in excitement as television showed the event. Never before had humans traveled so far from Earth or landed on another world.

The *Apollo 11* spacecraft had been sent into space by a giant *Saturn V* rocket, which gulped 15 tons of fuel per second and produced the thrust of 500 jet airplanes. The landing of the *Apollo 11* astronauts represented a fantastic moment in human history, and a great triumph for American science and technology.

President John F. Kennedy had challenged the nation in 1961 to reach the moon before the end of the decade. This was the response to the Soviet Union's success in sending a "cosmonaut" into orbit around the Earth. Years of effort and dozens of preliminary space flights paved the way for the historic flight of *Apollo 11*.

After a series of moon missions, the American space program sent unmanned craft to the outer reaches of the solar system. Space shuttles, which could go into orbit, return, and be launched again, carried out scientific studies while orbiting the Earth. By the mid-1990s, plans were under way to work with Russia in building a space station for long-term study of Earth's environment and the solar system.

The explosion of the *Challenger*.

THE CHALLENGER DISASTER

On January 28, 1986, just 72 seconds after liftoff from Cape Canaveral, Florida, the space shuttle *Challenger* exploded. All seven astronauts aboard were killed, as millions of horrified viewers watched on television. One of the astronauts was Christa McAuliffe, a teacher, who was the first private citizen chosen for a space flight.

EXPLORING THE SOLAR SYSTEM

The Hubble Space Telescope.

An important part of America's space program has been the use of unmanned spacecraft. The *Mariner,* for example, relayed to Earth detailed pictures of the surface of Mars, Venus, and Mercury. Other unmanned probes have explored Jupiter, Saturn, Uranus, and Neptune. And in 1990, the Hubble Space Telescope was launched into low Earth orbit. Free of the planet's atmosphere, the telescope provides a way to see far beyond the solar system.

95

THE VIETNAM WAR

THE COUNTRY DIVIDES AND DEBATES

A New York City demonstration against the Vietnam War.

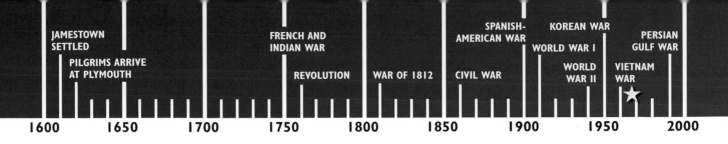

JAMESTOWN SETTLED

PILGRIMS ARRIVE AT PLYMOUTH

FRENCH AND INDIAN WAR

REVOLUTION

WAR OF 1812

SPANISH-AMERICAN WAR

CIVIL WAR

KOREAN WAR

WORLD WAR I

WORLD WAR II

PERSIAN GULF WAR

VIETNAM WAR

1600   1650   1700   1750   1800   1850   1900   1950   2000

- **1965 U.S. combat troops arrive in South Vietnam**
- **1968 Antiwar protests grow in strength**
- **1973 The last U.S troops leave South Vietnam**
- **1975 President Richard M. Nixon resigns The war ends as North Vietnamese forces defeat South Vietnam**

In the 1960s and 1970s, the United States was involved in a bitter war halfway around the world. In Southeast Asia, Vietnam was divided into two parts—South Vietnam and Communist North Vietnam. When Communist rebels backed by North Vietnam began a guerrilla war against South Vietnam, the United States sent aid and military advisors to the South.

By 1965, American troops were fighting a full-scale war against the rebels and regular North Vietnamese troops. Eventually, more than 600,000 U.S. troops were sent to fight in the Vietnam War, which spread to the nearby countries of Cambodia and Laos. Billions of dollars were spent on weapons. The U.S. government, and many Americans, believed that this huge effort was needed to stop the spread of communism.

But other Americans disagreed. They said that the conflict was really a civil war, and the United States had no right to be there. Antiwar protests began on college campuses. Students objected to the war and the military draft, which forced young men to serve in the army. By the late 1960s, many leaders in business, government, and society had joined the protest. They said that the war was not only wrong, but also unwinnable.

The United States negotiated a peace treaty with North Vietnam, and the last American troops left in 1973. Two years later, North Vietnamese forces took Saigon, the capital of South Vietnam. The war was finally over.

THREE ASSASSINATIONS

During the Vietnam War years, the United States was troubled by a series of tragic events that were unrelated to the war. None had a deeper effect on the country than the assassination of President John F. Kennedy. Kennedy was shot while riding in a motorcade in Dallas, Texas, on November 22, 1963. Because his assassin, Lee Harvey Oswald, was himself shot and killed before he could be tried, an air of mystery has long surrounded the assassination. Then, in 1968, the country reeled with the shock of two more killings of prominent Americans. Civil rights leader Martin Luther King, Jr., was shot in April. Ten weeks later, Robert F. Kennedy, the slain president's brother, was shot and killed while campaigning for the presidency.

PRESIDENT NIXON RESIGNS

While the Vietnam War was winding down, a scandal was unfolding in Washington, D.C. During the 1972 presidential campaign, a group of men working to re-elect President Richard M. Nixon were caught breaking into Democratic Party headquarters. Nixon tried to cover up their connection to the White House, but the truth came out, along with other campaign irregularities. Nixon was forced to resign in disgrace in August 1973, the first U.S. president ever to do so.

Richard M. Nixon bids farewell after resigning the presidency.

97

THE COMPUTER REVOLUTION

THE DAWN OF THE ELECTRONIC AGE

Early computers were huge and much less powerful than those of today.

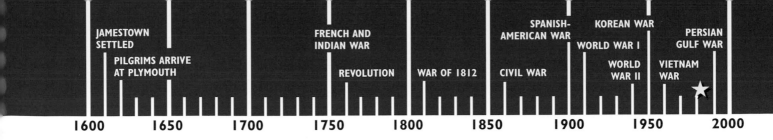

| JAMESTOWN SETTLED | | FRENCH AND INDIAN WAR | | | SPANISH-AMERICAN WAR | KOREAN WAR | PERSIAN GULF WAR |
| PILGRIMS ARRIVE AT PLYMOUTH | | REVOLUTION | WAR OF 1812 | CIVIL WAR | | WORLD WAR I / WORLD WAR II | VIETNAM WAR |

1600   1650   1700   1750   1800   1850   1900   1950   2000

- **1946 ENIAC is developed**
- **1978-1980 Personal computers are introduced**
- **1986 The first "megabit memory chip" holds 1 million bits of data**

Using a "laptop" computer.

In the early 1900s, the automobile and the airplane changed the way Americans lived. Then radio and television transformed their lives in other ways. Since 1980, the greatest engine of change has been the computer. ENIAC, the first electronic computer, was a huge machine that weighed 30 tons and contained 18,000 vacuum tubes. By the 1970s, tubes had been replaced by transistors and integrated circuits. And by the mid-1980s, computers were driven by tiny silicon "chips" imprinted with electronic circuits. Computers were small enough to fit in a briefcase—and more powerful than ever.

Computer technology is now routinely used to make machines and appliances run more efficiently. In industry, computerized robots perform assembly-line work. Corporations and governments often now use "supercomputers" that can carry out millions of instructions per second.

But perhaps the greatest impact on daily life in the United States has been the increasing use of personal computers (PCs) in schools, homes, and businesses. Desktop personal computers are used for everything from homework, to figuring a family budget, to calculating business profits. Computers are also creating new forms of entertainment through computer games and networks.

MEDICAL FRONTIERS

Some of the most exciting developments in the computer field are taking place in medical science. In "teleradiology," for example, a surgeon can send X-ray or CAT-scan pictures of a patient's brain to specialists in other parts of the world to get their opinions before operating. Computer imaging can also give medical scientists a way of examining a three-dimensional view of an organ such as the heart.

THE INFORMATION SUPERHIGHWAY

Computers are making new methods of communication possible. Many Americans are linking their computers to networks that allow them to send and receive information over telephone lines. They can get the latest news, research a report, order merchandise, or "chat" via computer with others. Eventually, many people believe that computer networks, telephone service, and cable television service will merge, linking homes and businesses in a giant network. The popular nickname for this network of the future is the "Information Superhighway."

Apple Computer founder Stephen Jobs (below left) and president John Scully (right).

A CHANGING WORLD

COMMUNISM FAILS AND THE COLD WAR ENDS

An unsuccessful attempt to overthrow Soviet president Mikhail Gorbachev occurred in the Soviet Union in August 1991.

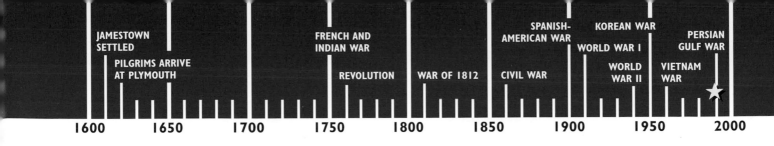

JAMESTOWN SETTLED		FRENCH AND INDIAN WAR			SPANISH-AMERICAN WAR	KOREAN WAR	PERSIAN GULF WAR
PILGRIMS ARRIVE AT PLYMOUTH						WORLD WAR I	
			REVOLUTION	WAR OF 1812	CIVIL WAR	WORLD WAR II	VIETNAM WAR

| 1600 | 1650 | 1700 | 1750 | 1800 | 1850 | 1900 | 1950 | 2000 |

- **1989-1991 Communism collapses in Eastern Europe and the Soviet Union**
- **1991 The Persian Gulf War is fought**
- **1994 U.S. troops enter Haiti, but war is avoided**

For more than 40 years after World War II, the United States had acted as leader of the "Free World" in the Cold War struggle against communism. Between 1989 and 1991, the Cold War ended as Communist regimes were replaced in Eastern Europe, and then in the Soviet Union. The Soviet Union itself split into independent republics, with Russia by far the largest and most influential.

In the 1990s, the United States was searching for a new world role. American foreign policy continued to be directed toward the country's traditional goals: world peace, human rights, and the right of people to choose their own government. Working toward these goals has sometimes involved the nation in trouble spots around the world.

American troops fought in the 1991 Persian Gulf War. They also took part in a mission to safeguard famine relief in Somalia, a country torn by civil war. And they led a peacekeeping mission in Haiti that paved the way for the return of the country's exiled president, Jean-Bertrand Aristide. The American government has also played a role in efforts to end conflicts in the Middle East and in the former Yugoslavia. As the United States moves toward the twenty-first century, it remains an important leader in an increasingly complicated world.

An Iraqi tank near Kuwait City during the Persian Gulf War.

THE EARTH DAY CHALLENGE

In the late 1960s, Americans began to worry about the environment. Pollution was everywhere. Natural resources were being wasted. Many species of wild animals and plants were dying out. One group of people decided to call attention to these problems with a special day—Earth Day—on April 22, 1970. About 20 million Americans took part in activities ranging from public protests to neighborhood cleanups. Earth Day helped make people aware of the environment, which led to laws designed to stop pollution, preserve resources, and save wildlife. But by 1990, it was clear that greater efforts were needed. Earth Day was revived, and it has been an annual event ever since. America and the world still face serious environmental problems, but thanks at least partly to Earth Day, more and more people are working to solve them.

THE PERSIAN GULF WAR

In 1990, the Persian Gulf nation of Iraq, ruled by dictator Saddam Hussein, invaded its tiny neighbor, the oil-rich kingdom of Kuwait. President George Bush persuaded 27 other countries to join the United States in demanding that Iraq withdraw from Kuwait. When Hussein refused, the American-led military forces launched "Desert Storm" on January 16, 1991. After weeks of powerful air strikes, a massive ground attack overwhelmed the Iraqi Army and liberated Kuwait. In this conflict, as in most others, the United States acted in cooperation with the United Nations.

c. 1000   Vikings reach the northeast coast of present-day Canada

1492   Christopher Columbus arrives in the "New World"

1513   Juan Ponce de León searches for the fountain of youth on a peninsula that he names Florida

1519–1521   The Spanish, led by Hernando Cortés, conquer the Aztec Empire

1540–1542   Francisco Vásquez de Coronado explores what is now known as the American Southwest

1565   St. Augustine is established

1587   The colony of Roanoke is settled by the British

1607   Jamestown is settled

1619   The House of Burgesses is established

Africans are brought to Virginia to work as indentured servants

1620   The Pilgrims establish the Plymouth colony in present-day Massachusetts

1621   The first Thanksgiving is celebrated

1630   Massachusetts Bay Colony is founded by the Puritans

1664   The British take over the Dutch colony of New Netherland; it becomes the colonies of New York and New Jersey

1681   William Penn invites people of all religions to come live in the new colony of Pennsylvania

1732   Benjamin Franklin publishes the first edition of *Poor Richard's Almanac*

1754   The French and Indian War begins

1759   The British capture Quebec

1763   Ottawa chief Pontiac leads a rebellion against the British

The 1763 Treaty of Paris ends the French and Indian War

King George III decrees that colonists cannot settle west of the Appalachian Mountains

1770   Five colonists are killed by British redcoats

1773   Colonists dump British tea into the Boston Harbor in protest of the British Tea Act

1774   Representatives from the colonies meet in Philadelphia for the First Continental Congress

1775   The Battles of Lexington and Concord begin the American Revolution

The Second Continental Congress meets and forms the Continental Army—George Washington is placed in command

The Battle of Bunker Hill takes place

1776   Thomas Paine publishes *Common Sense*

Thomas Jefferson writes most of the Declaration of Independence

The Second Continental Congress approves Jefferson's work on July 4

The British occupy New York City and Philadelphia

1777   The Patriots defeat the British in the Battle of Saratoga

George Washington's troops winter at Valley Forge

1781	Washington traps Cornwallis's troops at Yorktown, forcing the British surrender, and puts an end to the Revolution
1783	The British sign the Treaty of Paris, recognizing American independence
1787	Delegates to the Constitutional Convention create the U.S. Constitution
1789	George Washington is elected president
1791	The Bill of Rights is ratified
1793	Eli Whitney invents the cotton gin
1803	The United States buys the Louisiana Territory from France
	Thomas Jefferson sends ships to challenge the Barbary pirates in Tripoli
1804	Meriwether Lewis and William Clark begin to explore western North America
1807	Robert Fulton's *Cleremont* travels up the Hudson River
1812	America goes to war against Britain
1814	British troops set fire to government buildings in Washington, D.C.
	Francis Scott Key writes the "Star-Spangled Banner" after witnessing the bombardment of Fort McHenry
1815	General Andrew Jackson leads troops to victory at the Battle of New Orleans
1817	Construction begins on the Erie Canal
1821	Mexico wins independence from Spain
1836	Texans declare their independence from Mexico and declare the Republic of Texas
	Davy Crockett and Jim Bowie fight General Antonio López de Santa Anna at the Alamo
1837	Abolitionist Elijah P. Lovejoy is killed by a mob
1841	The first wagon train heads west to Oregon and California
1844	The first telegraph message is sent
1846	The United States declares war on Mexic
1847	Frederick Douglass begins publishing the *North Star*
1848	Gold is discovered at Sutter's Mill in California
1850	California becomes a state
	The Fugitive Slave Act is passed
1852	*Uncle Tom's Cabin,* by Harriet Beecher Stowe, is published
1860	The Pony Express is formed
1861	The Civil War begins
	Confederates win the First Battle of Bull Run
1862	The *Monitor* and the *Merrimack* battle
	Confederates win the Second Battle of Bull Run
	The Union wins the Battle of Antietam
	Abraham Lincoln issues the Emancipation Proclamation
	The Homestead Act offers settlers 160 acresof land for free
1863	The Battle of Gettysburg takes place
1865	General Robert E. Lee surrenders to General Ulysses S. Grant at Appomattox Court House
	Abraham Lincoln is assassinated by John Wilkes Booth
	The Thirteenth Amendment to the Constitution is ratified by the states, ending slavery forever
1867	William H. Seward arranges the Alaska Purchase
1869	The Union Pacific and Central Pacific Railroads meet in Utah
	The U. S. government begins to place all Native Americans on reservations
1876	The Battle of Little Big Horn is fought
1890	More than 200 Sioux die at Wounded Knee

1869	Wyoming Territory gives women the right to vote
1872	Susan B. Anthony is arrested for voting
1876	Alexander Graham Bell invents the telephone
1877	Thomas Edison invents the phonograph
1879	Edison invents the lightbulb
1880	Immigrants begin to arrive in America by the millions
1886	The Statue of Liberty is dedicated
	The American Federation of Labor is formed
1895	Edison shows the first moving picture
1898	The United States declares war on Spain
	Hawaii becomes a U. S. territory
1903	Mother Jones leads 300 child workers on a protest march
	Wilbur and Orville Wright complete the first airplane flight
1913	Henry Ford uses an assembly line to produce automobiles
1914	The Panama Canal opens
1917	The United States enters World War I
1919	The Eighteenth Amendment, prohibiting the production or sale of alcohol, is passed
1920	The Nineteenth Amendment gives the vote to women
1927	Charles A. Lindbergh flies nonstop across the Atlantic
1929	The stock market collapses
1933	Dust storms begin in the Great Plains
1941	Pearl Harbor is bombed; America enters World War II
1945	The United States drops atomic bombs on Hiroshima and Nagasaki; World War II ends
1946	The "baby boom" begins as veterans of World War II come home
	The first electronic computer is created
1950	The Korean War begins
1953	Dr. Jonas Salk announces the creation of the polio vaccine
1954	The U. S. Supreme Court declares segregated schools unconstitutional
1955	Rosa Parks is arrested for refusing to give up her seat on a bus to a white man
1956	The U. S. government launches the interstate highway system
1957	The Soviet Union launches *Sputnik I*
1960s	The United States becomes involved in the war in Vietnam
1961	The Berlin Wall divides Berlin, Germany, into east and west
1962	Rachel Carson's *Silent Spring* is published
	The Cuban Missile Crisis takes place
1963	More than 200,000 civil rights supporters march in Washington, D. C.
	John F. Kennedy is assassinated
1968	Martin Luther King, Jr., is assassinated
	Robert F. Kennedy is assassinated
1969	*Apollo 11* lands on the moon
1973	U.S. combat troops leave South Vietnam
	Richard M. Nixon becomes the first U. S. president to resign
1986	The space shuttle *Challenger* explodes after liftoff from Cape Canaveral
1991	The Persian Gulf War is fought

Barrett, Tracy. *Growing Up in Colonial America.* Brookfield, CT: The Millbrook Press, 1995.

Beller, Susan P. *Medical Practices in the Civil War.* Cincinnati, OH: Shoe Tree Press, 1992.

Black, Wallace B., and Blashfield, Jean F. *D-Day.* New York: Macmillan Children's Book Group, 1992.

Branley, Franklyn M. *From Sputnik to Space Shuttle: Into the New Space Age.* New York: HarperCollins Children's Books, 1986.

Brownstone, David M., and Franck, Irene M. *Historic Places of Early America.* New York: Macmillan, 1989.

Fisher, Margaret, and Fowler, Mary J., editors. *Colonial America: English Colonies.* Grand Rapids, MI: Gateway Press, Inc., 1988.

Foster, Leila M. *The Story of the Persian Gulf War.* Chicago: Childrens Press, 1991.

Fraser, Mary A. *One Giant Leap.* New York: Henry Holt & Co., 1993.

Hargrove, Jim. *Abraham Lincoln.* Chicago: Childrens Press, 1988.

Hauptly, Denis J. *A Convention of Delegates: The Creation of the Constitution.* New York: Macmillan Children's Book Group, 1987.

Hills, Ken. *World War Two.* New York: Marshall Cavendish, 1988.

Johnson, Hilda S. *A Child's Diary—The 1930's.* Studley, VA: The Wishing Room, Inc., 1988.

Kallen, R. *Building A Nation* (series). Minneapolis, MN: Abdo and Daughters Press, 1992.

Kent, Zachary. *The Story of the Rough Riders.* Chicago: Childrens Press, 1991.

King, David C. *America's Story* (series). Littleton, MA: Sundance Publishing Co., 1982, 1995.

Kroll, Steven. Lewis and Clark: *Explorers of the Far West.* New York: Holiday House, Inc., 1994.

Lyngheim, Linda. *Gold Rush Adventure.* Chatsworth, CA: Langtry Publications, 1988.

McCall, Edith. *Frontiers of America* (series). Chicago: Childrens Press, 1980.

McGovern, Ann. *The Secret Soldier: The Story of Deborah Sampson.* New York: Scholastic, Inc., 1990.

Olesky, Walter. *The Boston Tea Party*. New York: Franklin Watts, Inc., 1993.

Oneal, Zibby. *A Long Way to Go*. New York: Viking Children's Books, 1990.

Osborne, Mary P. *The Many Lives of Benjamin Franklin*. New York: Dial Books for Young Readers, 1990.

Patterson, Lillie. *Frederick Douglass: Freedom Fighter*. New York: Chelsea House, 1991.

Rappaport, Doreen. *Escape from Slavery: Five Journeys to Freedom*. New York: HarperCollins Children's Books, 1991.

Roop, Peter, and Roop, Connie. *Off the Map: The Journals of Lewis and Clark*. New York: Walker and Co., 1993.

Sabin, Francene. *American Revolution*. Mahwah, NJ: Troll Associates, 1985.

Skipper, G. C. *Pearl Harbor*. Chicago: Childrens Press, 1983.

Stein, R. Conrad. *Ellis Island*. Chicago: Childrens Press, 1992.

_____. *The Story of the Erie Canal*. Chicago: Childrens Press, 1985.

_____. *The Story of the Great Depression*. Chicago: Childrens Press, 1985.

Weiner, Eric. *The Civil War*. New York: Smithmark Publishers, Inc., 1993.

Wright, David K. *War in Vietnam* (series). Chicago: Childrens Press, 1989.

Photo Credits

Cover photos: (clockwise from top) Buzz Aldrin on the moon, National Aeronautics and Space Administration; Christopher Columbus, North Wind Picture Archives; Franklin D. Roosevelt, ©The Bettmann Archive; Suffrage march, Library of Congress; Signing of the Constitution, National Archives.

Contents photos (top to bottom): Page 4: Mayflower Compact, North Wind Picture Archives; George Washington at Yorktown, North Wind Picture Archives; Panning for gold, North Wind Picture Archives. Page 5: Abraham Lincoln, National Portrait Gallery; Soup kitchen line, National Archives; Buzz Aldrin on the moon, National Aeronautics and Space Administration.

Pages 11 (left), 12, 13, 14, 15, 16, 17, 18, 19, 20, 25, 28, 29, 30, 31 (left), 36, 37 (right), 38, 39, 40, 41, 42, 44, 45, 46, 47, 52, 59 (top), 62, 70: North Wind Picture Archives; pages 10, 32, 53 (left): National Portrait Gallery; pages 6, 8, 9, 11 (right), 22, 23, 24, 26, 31 (right), 33, 34, 35, 48, 55, 56, 57, 61 (left), 63 (right), 68, 69, 72, 76, 77: Library of Congress; pages 23, 27 (left), 54, 71, 74, 75, 78, 80, 82, 83, 84, 85 (bottom), 91, 92: National Archives; page 27 (right): U. S. Bureau of Engraving and Printing; pages 37 (left), 49, 67 (top), 99 (right): ©Blackbirch Press, Inc.; page 43: Woolaroc Museum, Bartlesville, Oklahoma; pages 51, 53, 58, 60, 61 (right), 64, 66, 79, 88, 95 (bottom): ©The Bettmann Archive; pages 59 (bottom), 63 (left), 67 (bottom), 81, 85 (top), 86, 96, 98: ©AP/Wide World Photos; pages 73, 88, 93, 97: ©UPI/Bettmann; page 90: John Fitzgerald Kennedy Library; page 93: National Aeronautics and Space Administration; pages 95 (top), 99 (left), 100: Gamma Liaison; page 101: Reuters/Bettmann.